An Introduction to Career Learning and Development 11–19

An Introduction to Career Learning and Development 11–19 is an indispensible source of support and guidance for all those who need to know why and how career learning and development should be planned, developed and delivered effectively to meet the needs of young people.

It is a comprehensive resource providing a framework for career education conducive with the realities of lifelong learning, enterprise, flexibility and resilience in a dynamic world. It discusses the key underpinning theory and policies and provides straightforward, practical advice for students and practising professionals. Experts in the field provide essential guidance on:

- development and leadership of career education strategies in school
- planning and implementing career learning activities in the curriculum
- collaborative working and engagement between schools, colleges and careers and guidance services, as well as with parents, community and business organisations
- key organisations and where to find useful resources
- effective teaching and learning – active, participative and experiential learning approaches
- issues of ethics, values, equality and diversity
- guidance on self-evaluation, making the most of inspection, and quality standards and awards.

An Introduction to Career Learning and Development 11–19 is an invaluable guide for teachers, teaching support staff, career guidance professionals and all other partners in the delivery of careers education information advice and guidance (CEIAG) who wish to enhance their understanding of current and emerging practice and provide support that can really make a difference to young people's lives.

Anthony Barnes is Visiting Senior Lecturer at the Centre for Career and Personal Development, Canterbury Christ Church University and Careers Education and IAG Consultant, Babcock, UK.

Dr Barbara Bassot is Programme Director for the MA in Career Guidance at the Centre for Career and Personal Development, Canterbury Christ Church University, UK.

Anne Chant is Course Director for the Advanced Certificate in Careers Education and Guidance at the Centre for Career and Personal Development, Canterbury Christ Church University, UK.

The landscape of education and training that we are asking young people to navigate is becoming more complex. At the same time changes in the economy mean that the opportunities in work are constantly evolving. More than ever before young people need to develop the skills to plan and manage their journey through learning and work – to learn about career and to learn for their career.

The authors of *Career Learning and Development* have drawn on their collective experiences, as careers practitioners and lecturers on courses for careers leaders in schools, to produce a timely resource book that should be essential reading for anyone involved in leading, delivering and developing programmes of careers education in schools and colleges. It is both a textbook, with extensive references to sources of further reading, and a practical handbook with several useful planning and review tools and suggestions for activities with young people. At its core is good practice, underpinned by theory and informed by research. It encourages the reader to reflect on their practice and looks to possible developments for the future.

The careers workforce itself is changing, with more than one in four schools now having a careers coordinator from a background other than teaching. All recently appointed careers coordinators should read this book but more experienced practitioners will also find the final chapters challenging and inspiring.

David Andrews OBE, *Faculty of Education, University of Cambridge*

This is the perfect companion for anyone working in the field of career learning and development who is interested in extending their professionalism, but feels they don't have time to engage with the thinking, or don't know how to source relevant reading. This book is a substantial resource in one volume.

Beginning with an introduction to the theoretical underpinning of career-learning and development, it goes on to offer a myriad of ideas for classroom practice, and ends with a look at strategic planning and future development.

It makes theory read like a guide to good practice, is full of helpful hints throughout the text for improving day to day delivery, has key questions at the end of each chapter to help focus on individual settings, and provides extensive references to further reading if, and when, this will be manageable.

Everything is presented in bite-sized chunks, from ideas that can be thought about on the way to work, and small steps that need take only a few minutes to set up, through to frameworks that can form the basis for partner discussions and outline a development programme. Despite this, the book cleverly avoids a micro-management approach, and leaves space that invites professional creativity.

The authors recognise that most of us will need to dip in and out of the book according to need, so have helpfully cross-referenced key ideas, concepts and practice throughout - so whatever the start point the built-in links to other relevant sections offer potential enrichment when the time, relevance and opportunities are there.

There is something here for everyone at any stage of their role and responsibility for career learning and development.

Barbara McGowan, *Senior Fellow, National Institute for Career Education and Counselling (NICEC)*

An Introduction to Career Learning and Development 11–19

Perspectives, practice and possibilities

Anthony Barnes, Barbara Bassot and Anne Chant

Routledge
Taylor & Francis Group

LONDON AND NEW YORK

This first edition published 2011
by Routledge
2 Park Square, Milton Park, Abingdon, Oxon, OX14 4RN

Simultaneously published in the USA and Canada
by Routledge
270 Madison Avenue, New York, NY 10016

Routledge is an imprint of the Taylor & Francis Group, an informa business

Typeset in Galliard by Swales & Willis Ltd, Exeter, Devon
Printed and bound in Great Britain by TJ International Ltd, Padstow, Cornwall

British Library Cataloguing in Publication Data
A catalogue record for this book is available from the British Library

Library of Congress Cataloging-in-Publication Data
Barnes, Anthony, 1949–
    An introduction to career learning and development, 11–19 /
Anthony Barnes, Barbara Bassot, and Anne Chant.
    p. cm.
    Includes bibliographical references and index.
    1. Career education—Great Britain.
    2. Career development—Great Britain.
    I. Bassot, Barbara. II. Chant, Anne. III. Title.
    LC1037.8.G7B37 2011
    370.11'3—dc22
    2010013650

ISBN13: 978–0–415–57777–9 (hbk)
ISBN13: 978–0–415–57778–6 (pbk)
ISBN13: 978–0–203–84187–7 (ebk)

Contents

Acknowledgements

We would like to thank our families, colleagues and students for the inspiration they gave us; and we would especially like to express our thanks to Phil Bassot for his excellent work in producing the diagrams and to Marc Bassot for his careful proof reading. Chapter 11 and part of the Introduction are published with kind permission of the Institute of Career Guidance, Stourbridge. They first appeared as Bassot (2009) *Career Learning and Development: A Bridge to the Future*, in the ICG's biennial research publication entitled Constructing the Future: Career Guidance for Changing Contexts, edited by Hazel Reid. It is available from http://www.icg-uk.org/ICG_publicatons.html

Abbreviations

ACEG	Association for Careers Education and Guidance
ADHD	Attention Deficit and Hyperactivity Disorder
BTEC	A brand of work-related qualifications offered by Edexcel
CASVE	Communication, Analysis, Synthesis, Valuing, Execution
CBI	Confederation of British Industry
CEG	Careers Education and Guidance
CEIAG	Careers Education, Information, Advice and Guidance
CIP	Cognitive Information Processing
CLD	Career Learning and Development
CV	Curriculum Vitae
DCSF	Department for Children, Schools and Families
DfE	Department for Education
DfES	Department for Education and Science
DOTS	Decision learning, Opportunity awareness, Transition learning, Self awareness
DTI	Department for Trade and Industry
ECM	Every Child Matters
EFFE	Essential Foundation and Fundamental Entitlement
EI	Emotional Intelligence
FE	Further Education
GCSE	General Certificate of Secondary Education
GNVQ	General National Vocational Qualification
HE	Higher Education
HRM	Human resource management
IAG	Information, Advice and Guidance
ICG	Institute of Career Guidance
ICT	Information and Communication Technology
IES	Institute for Employment Studies
INSET	In Service Training
IQ	Intelligence Quotient
IT	Information Technology
LA	Local Authority
LEA	Local Education Authority
National College	National College for Leadership of Schools and Children's Services
NCC	National Curriculum Council
NEET	Not in Education, Employment or Training

NFER	National Foundation for Educational Research
NIACE	National Institute of Adult Continuing Education
NICEC	National Institute for Careers Education and Counselling
NOCN	National Open College Network
OCD	Obsessive Compulsive Disorder
Ofsted	Office for Standards in Education, Children's Services and Skills
PE	physical education
PD	personal development
PEP	personal education plan
PSHEe	Personal, Social, Health and Economic education
PLTS	Personal, Learning and Thinking Skills
QCA	Qualifications and Curriculum Authority
QCDA	Qualifications and Curriculum Development Agency
RE	Religious Education
RoSLA	Raising of the School Leaving Age
SCAA	School Curriculum and Assessment Authority
SENCO	Special Educational Needs Coordinator
SESIFU	Sensing, Sifting, Focusing and Understanding
SMART	Specific, Measurable, Achievable, Realistic and Time-bound
STEM	Science, Technology, Engineering and Maths
SWOT	Strengths, Weaknesses, Opportunities and Threats
TAEN	Age and Employment Network
TUC	Trades Union Congress
TVEI	Technical and Vocational Education Initiative
TVEE	Technical and Vocational Education Extension
WRL	Work-Related Learning
WRLE	Work-Related Learning and Enterprise
ZPD	Zone of Proximal Development

Introduction

This book is written for all those who need to know why and how career learning and development can be planned, developed and delivered effectively to meet the needs of young people. Some will have roles and titles including careers coordinator, head of careers, careers adviser or careers teacher. They could also include undergraduate and postgraduate students on relevant courses and others with a more academic interest in the area. In addition, many careers personal advisers and other partners in the delivery of careers education information advice and guidance (CEIAG) will find it useful.

The origins of this book are in the collaboration between the authors on teaching the Advanced Certificate in Careers Education and Guidance at Canterbury Christ Church University. The context of the book, therefore, is England, but many of the ideas and approaches have a general application and we have made reference to international developments where appropriate.

Calls for new models for careers work in the twenty-first century

There is no doubt that the nature of work is changing at a rapid pace in response to the impact of ICT and globalised marketplaces. The continued use of traditional models with an emphasis on matching people to jobs has been questioned. As a result, there have been calls for new models that are 'fit for purpose' for careers work in the twenty-first century.

To inform the writing of Section 8 of the Skills Commission's Report *Inspiration and Aspiration: Realising our Potential in the 21st Century*, a number of experts (including Professor Jenny Bimrose) were consulted to gain their views on the models currently used by those involved in careers education and guidance (CEG). The following comment from the report summarises these:

> Professor Bimrose said that in various forms, the matching model has remained the dominant influence on guidance since the model's formulation in the first decade of the 20th century. She and other experts said that there is an urgent need to recognise that the matching model is flawed. Professor Bimrose described the matching model as 'a hundred years out of date' and Gareth Dent, former Head of Advice and E-services at University for Industry (Ufi), argued that 'it is important that we move beyond this approach'.
>
> (Skills Commission 2008: 20)

The report goes on to examine some of the problems with the matching model. This includes a discussion of its suitability for a more stable time when the labour market was less complex, when people often made career decisions at the start of their working lives and often did not then need to review them later in life. It also points to the desire of many individuals today to be flexible, rather than have a career for life, and to make autonomous decisions, rather than be matched to a career by an adviser. The section concludes with the strongly worded recommendation that:

> The Government must recognise that IAG is often provided using outdated delivery models and that IAG services will become increasingly irrelevant unless this changes.
>
> (Skills Commission 2008: 21)

The report suggests that professionals involved in careers work need to have a knowledge and understanding of theoretical approaches, in particular of recent approaches. There is no doubt that traditional approaches have aided those in career guidance for many years, but there is also a need for new approaches that fit twenty-first-century life. Otherwise, careers work runs the risk of being seen as outdated at best and irrelevant at worst. The need for new models, therefore, appears to be beyond question.

Problems with terminology

Since the statutory Careers Service came into being in the UK in the 1970s, professional practitioners in the field have been given job titles such as careers officers, careers advisers and, more recently in Connexions services in England, personal advisers. The term favoured in recent policy documents on the subject of career guidance with young people and until recently with adults (DCSF 2007; International Centre for Guidance Studies 2008) is Information, Advice and Guidance (IAG) advisers. The terminology being used is problematic for the following reasons.

First, the term 'Information' is difficult as it implies that if people have good, up-to-date information, they will be able to make informed decisions. In practice, this is often not the case as reading information can often mean that people become confused. In addition, the question of how people can make a career decision simply by reading about occupations remains unanswered.

Second, the term 'Advice' is also problematic as it implies receiving wisdom from an expert. In general, people have contact with an adviser when they need specialised information and are seeking direction regarding a course of action. Advice is usually based on the recognition of need by the person concerned. The individual expects the adviser, as an expert, to direct them to the best way forward. In relation to people seeking careers advice, the term implies that they already know what they want ('a career as a . . .') and are seeking advice on how to get there from an expert who is more knowledgeable than they are and who is able to show them the best route.

Third, the term 'Guidance' similarly presents difficulties. The word guidance implies that there is someone guiding or leading and another being guided. When using the term in relation to career, again the notion of a knowledgeable expert, who will lead the way so that people can follow, is implied.

All the above means that the term IAG is problematic, not least because it implies that the onus is on the professional to show the student the way forward. Often the easiest way of achieving this (and indeed what many students expect in the light of the terminology being used) is by using the matching model.

In today's society, people need to be able to cope with turbulent labour markets, where career opportunities and individual lives can change in an ongoing and sometimes rapid way. If people are to manage such change, they need a model focused on learning and adapting to what the future may bring.

From positivism to constructivism

During the late 1990s there was a move from the idea of a 'career for life' to a career being something that individuals construct throughout their lives (Collin and Young 2000). During much of the previous century, the terms 'career' and 'work', or more particularly 'paid work', were seen as synonymous. The commonly used matching model could be seen as falling within the positivist paradigm, where the concrete reality of a career for life was sought.

In the later part of the twentieth century, the notion of a job for life was called into question, not least because of times of economic recession. The impact of globalisation and the use of ICT were further factors in creating constant and rapid change in people's experiences of career. The need for people to be able to navigate a career pathway through life grew in prominence. Positivist traditions with their emphasis on rational planning, ideally suited to stable environments, began to be rejected in favour of constructivist approaches, where the client is an active participant in the process of constructing their career throughout their lives (McMahon and Patton 2006).

What is career learning and development?

Career learning and development (hereafter CLD) offers a different model with a distinctly alternative theoretical orientation to that of the positivist matching approach. The term 'CLD' was first used by Bassot (2009) and is built on the principles of social constructivism (Bassot 2006), which, when applied to careers work, emphasises that knowledge about career is not simply acquired; people are not 'empty vessels' that can be 'filled up' with career information, on the assumption that professionals can advise or guide them into making decisions. By contrast, CLD asserts that knowledge about career is constructed through activity and in interactions with a variety of people (including career professionals, employers, teachers, parents and peers). Individuals need ongoing experiences and opportunities for discussion in order to construct this knowledge within their changing social and cultural context. CLD happens throughout people's lives, as they continue to develop their knowledge and skills and adapt to the changing labour market.

Terminology in the field of careers work varies in time and space, which can be especially confusing for those who are new to it. In this book, we have used the term 'CLD', but as and when the context requires it, we have also used these terms with the following meanings:

- *Career(s) education* – teaching and learning for the intentional promotion of CLD. This term has been used widely in England from the 1970s onwards. In the 1990s, it became fashionable to drop the 's' to emphasise that the activity is about the individual career rather than the world of careers.
- *Information, Advice and Guidance (IAG)* – as discussed previously. The term 'IAG' originated in the adult guidance sector in the 1990s and was taken up by the secondary sector in the early part of the first decade of this century. This happened at the time when it dropped out of use with those who work with adults, who found the terms

impenetrable. Sometimes, IAG is prefaced with the word 'careers' to distinguish career-related IAG from general IAG. Career(s) guidance continues to exist alongside the term 'IAG'.

- *Careers education, information, advice and guidance (CEIAG)* – the overarching term used for the arrangements to provide career-related teaching and learning and support for individuals in a school. This became widespread in the second half of the first decade of this century. It overtook the term 'careers education and guidance (CEG)', which became fashionable in the late 1980s.

Readers will be able to make sense of other variants that can be found in the literature; for example, career learning, information, advice and guidance (CLIAG) in the Further Education sector, careers and the world of work (CWoW) in Wales. Terminology changes rapidly; for example we are aware that Looked After Children (LAC) are in some areas now referred to as Children Looked After (CLA). In such instances, we urge readers not to be distracted and to focus on the general meaning of terms rather than their specific labels.

In the text, we also refer to children (up to age 11) and young people in a collective sense. We call them learners when we are focusing on CLD; and we call them pupils (up to age 16) and students (beyond age 16) in a school setting.

Purpose

The purpose of this book is threefold. First, it provides a resource for those who lead or support the development and delivery of CLD in secondary sector schools. However, in concentrating on this age group of students we are not suggesting that those who are younger or older cannot and will not benefit from learning about career. Indeed, the DCSF was interested in exploring the potential benefits of career learning for younger children (DCSF, 2009) and in developing an all-age career guidance service in England (as they have already been developed in other countries of the United Kingdom). Parts of this book will be helpful to those engaged with the primary sector, Further and Higher Education and those who work with adults. In writing this book, we have put together a comprehensive source to enable professionals to meet the needs of young people as they prepare to enter a rapidly changing world of work.

Second, the book aims to support the continuing professional development of the leaders and deliverers of careers work. Its roots are in the design of an accredited course which meets the requirements of the National Framework for Professional Qualifications in CEG (CEIAG Support Programme 2008).

Third, the book looks to the future development of programmes of CLD and also to the continued evolution of our understanding of it into new and innovative models and frameworks.

Structure

The book is divided into three sections: Perspectives, Practice and Possibilities. In Part A we look at CLD from three perspectives. Chapter 1 considers some of the theoretical approaches to career that have underpinned many of the developments in the field over the years, and have shaped what we understand of the CLD needs of young people and how we might best meet them. We begin the book with theoretical perspectives because it is only when we have a shared understanding of the subject that we can then move forward to build on what has already been achieved. That common understanding begins with the fundamental question of what we mean by the term 'career' and goes on to compare and contrast ideas and models of how career can be understood and supported. Chapter 2 focuses on how practitioners can engage with research. It explores the relationship of research to theory, policy and practice. Chapter 3, the final one in Part A, examines the response of policy-makers and the various drivers of policies relevant to CLD. There is no doubt that education in general can be seen as a political tool, and CLD is a stark example of this, as it operates at the interface between education and society.

In Part B, we turn to the practice of CLD. This is the largest part of the book and in it we explore the practicalities of developing and delivering a CLD programme for young people in school or college. Chapter 4 introduces the importance and challenges of the leadership of CLD within an organisation, taking a strategic look at the management of personnel, resources and timetabling. The key word in this chapter is 'leadership' and its impact on the development of programmes and schemes of work. In Chapter 5 we look more closely at the design of such programmes and models of delivery, such as the use of cross-curriculum themes, integration with other areas of personal development learning and the relative merits of designated or dedicated career lessons. Chapter 6 focuses on what young people need to learn in CLD programmes. Taking into consideration the frameworks, standards and guidance available, we return to the essence of CLD and examine the Essential Foundation that should be the Fundamental Entitlement (EFFE) for all young people. In our exploration of EFFE, we capture the essence of several relevant frameworks. We acknowledge that the needs of all young people are not the same and that some learners have additional issues that must be considered. In Chapter 7, we examine the needs of a range of young people with challenging issues. This includes those who are gifted and talented, those with disabilities and additional needs and those with more complex social and emotional issues. We suggest provision additional to EFFE and the support that can be designed around the particular needs of these students.

In the last three chapters of Part B, we turn to topics that ensure that the delivery of CLD does not stand still, but continues to improve and evolve alongside the needs of the learners, tapping into the networks that can support and enhance it. Chapter 8 takes a critical look at staff development. We look closely at the importance of the continuing development of staff within the context of the wider delivery teams in schools and colleges and within professional bodies. Such rigour in professional development is built upon in Chapter 9, in which we consider the importance of the maintenance of continual improvement procedures illustrated by quality improvement systems, standards and quality kite marks. Chapter 10 is the last chapter in Part B and explores the importance of partnership working, in order to maximise the content, impact and scope of CLD. Partners here are not limited to those formalised by government or local authority structures. They include and encourage informal partnerships with parents/carers, communities, voluntary groups and, of course, the young people themselves.

In Part C, we look to the possibilities that the future may bring. In Chapter 11 we introduce a new model for CLD, the need for which will be discussed later in this introduction. The model uses the metaphor of a suspension bridge (Bassot 2009) between learning and the world of work and examines all its essential component parts. Each part is vital to the effective functioning of the bridge, as is the balance between them. This model offers leaders of CLD a comprehensive platform on which to develop their provision. Such programmes need to be fit for the purpose of preparing young people for their adult lives in the twenty-first century. This work needs to be done not in a simplistic, linear, age-based fashion, but in a way that is conducive with the realities and necessities of lifelong learning, enterprise and risk taking, flexibility and resilience in a dynamic and rapidly changing world. The book culminates with Chapter 12, where we offer some examples of activities in the classroom and elsewhere that could be used to construct each of the components of the CLD bridge.

How to use this book

This book has been designed to start with the foundations of CLD and to move logically from theory to practice and on to future developments. We would like to recommend that this is indeed the order in which you will engage with it. However, it is clear that many of the potential readers of this book may not have the luxury of doing so, and therefore we invite you to approach it in which ever way meets your needs. In doing so you will sometimes be referred back to earlier chapters and on to later ones and we urge you to follow those referrals if at all possible.

At the end of each chapter we offer some discussion points for you to consider yourself or to share with others. In particular, you may find that these discussions can be used to shape the direction of discussions within a learning environment or in the context of a careers team.

We trust that you will find the book useful and enjoyable in your quest to engage a wide range of young people in their CLD.

References

Bassot, B. (2006) 'Constructing new understandings of career guidance: joining the dots' in H.L. Reid and J. Bimrose (eds) *Constructing the Future IV: Transforming Career Guidance*, Stourbridge: Institute of Career Guidance.

Bassot, B. (2009) 'Career learning and development: a bridge to the future' in H.L. Reid (ed) *Constructing the Future: Career Guidance for Changing Contexts*, Stourbridge: Institute of Career Guidance. Online: http: www.icg-uk.org/ICG_publications.html (accessed 14 February 2010).

CEIAG Support Programme (2008) *National Framework for Professional Qualifications in CEG*. Online: www.cegnet.co.uk/files/CEGNET0001/resources/586.doc (accessed 13 February 2010).

Collin, A. and Young, R.A. (2000) *The Future of Career*, Cambridge: Cambridge University Press.

DCSF (2007) *Quality Standards for Young People's Information Advice and Guidance (IAG)*, Sheffield: DCSF. Online. http://www.cegnet.co.uk/files/CEGNET0001/ManagingCEG/QualityStandardsforIAG/quality_standards_young_people.pdf (accessed 12 Feb-ruary 2010).

DCSF (2009) *Quality, Choice and Aspiration. A Strategy for Young People's Information, Advice and Guidance*. Online: www.publications.dcsf.gov.uk/eOrderingDownload/IAG-Report-v2.pdf (accessed 12 February 2010).

International Centre for Guidance Studies (2008) *Cross Government Review of Information Advice & Guidance Services for Adults in England*, Derby: University of Derby. Online: www.iagreview.org.uk/keydocs/IAG%20Review%20in%20England%20Final%20Report%20140308%20jh.pdf (accessed 12 February 2010).

McMahon, M. and Patton, W. (2006) *Career Counselling: Constructivist Approaches*, Abingdon: Routledge.

Skills Commission (2008) *Inspiration and Aspiration: Realising our Potential in the 21st Century*, London: Skills Commission. Online: www.policyconnect.org.uk/fckimages/Insprration%20and%20Aspiration.pdf (accessed 12 February 2010)

Part A

Perspectives

Chapter 1

Theoretical perspectives

In writing this chapter, we decided to focus on a small number of theoretical approaches that we felt would be useful to you as professionals working in the CLD area to help enhance your knowledge and understanding in relation to your work. The chapter begins with a consideration of the meaning of the concept of career and gives some insights into the continuing relevance of traditional theoretical approaches. It then examines some more recent approaches and what they have to offer to the continuing debate about career. The chapter concludes with a discussion of the reasons why an understanding of theory is important for those who are helping young people to learn about their future. This chapter is by no means exhaustive and inevitably there are other theories that we have excluded. We hope that by reading this chapter you may be prompted to read more to extend your knowledge and understanding and at various points we give you suggestions for further reading.

What do we mean by 'career'? The past, present and future

The word 'career' is used regularly in everyday conversation and is a word that most people think they probably understand. For many, the words 'work' and 'career' are synonymous, and the word 'work' to many will mean paid work as distinct from work in a more general sense. As a professional involved in CLD, it is important to be clear about your own understanding of the terms 'work' and 'career' and to be able to communicate these to those you are seeking to help.

In the middle of the twentieth century, people generally used the word 'career' to mean some form of paid work that they entered after they left education (often at the end of compulsory schooling) and stayed in for a considerable length of time, perhaps even for the duration of their working lives. Work often started with some form of apprenticeship or traineeship generally on low pay to start with, but with structured progression built in to allow people to gain more knowledge and skills and become more effective in the workplace. Following this, some progressed up a hierarchy within an organisation via promotion opportunities involving more responsibility. This perception of career largely described the male experience of work.

During the late 1970s and 1980s, the structure of the UK labour market began to change as many manufacturing industries struggled to compete in global markets. The car industry is one example of an industry that almost collapsed following competition from cheaper high-quality goods being imported from overseas, namely Japan. Many other UK manufacturing industries suffered similar fates and over a period of approximately twenty years, a move from an economy based on manufacturing to one based on the service sector is evident. As employers struggled to compete in the increasingly global market place, many stopped investing in training (often the first thing to go when times are hard), and apprenticeships became few and far between. This trend was exacerbated by the demise of most of the Industry Training Boards: the bodies with a responsibility to oversee training in particular industries.

Today we can see the evidence of these fundamental economic changes in our local communities. One such example is Chatham Maritime in north Kent. Until 1979, Chatham dockyard was in full operation, manufacturing a range of ships for the Royal Navy. Each year the dockyard offered 250 craft apprenticeships in a range of skilled trades and many apprentices would spend the whole of their working lives progressing up a hierarchy of opportunities within the dockyard. In 1979, the proposed closure of the dockyard was announced and the recruitment of new apprentices stopped immediately, prior to its closure in 1984. The dockyard was only one of a number of large employers in the area that undertook such action as the whole of north Kent plunged into deep recession. Today, huge changes have taken place and the area is in the process of being regenerated. The dockyard itself is now the Historic Dockyard, attracting thousands of visitors each year. The area surrounding it has become a retail park and there are campuses for three local universities all working together to ensure a good supply of skilled labour in the region. The disappearance of large numbers of apprenticeships has meant that opportunities for young people in the area have changed significantly, with a large majority now staying on in further and higher education.

It is all too easy to paint a rosy picture of the impact of economic changes such as those described above and for many young people the disappearance of apprenticeships means that they enter some of the four million low-skilled jobs that the UK economy now requires. These are often poorly paid jobs within the service sector with relatively few opportunities for advancement (Roberts 2005). The advent of 'apprenticeships' has done something to compensate for this, although access to such opportunities is highly competitive, as Unwin and Wellington (2001) discovered. Although this research is now somewhat dated, their findings are still relevant. As many more people study at university level, questions arise about the nature of work that these students gain, as fewer enter what could be termed graduate jobs in an ever-more competitive market. This is particularly the case for women (Walker and Zhu 2005). However, in the global market place highly skilled and innovative people are needed to enable us as a nation to compete on an equal footing. As a result, the world of careers work has become full of dilemmas and contradictions, giving much food for thought for those engaged in CLD.

Like any other area of life in this world of rapid change, the future of career is difficult to predict. Some writers (Edwards 1993; Storey 2000) have suggested that change is so prevalent and rapid that the whole notion of a career with progression up a hierarchy is outdated and that in our postmodern society flexible workers are needed. Such workers can transfer their skills and knowledge from one contract to the next as new business is generated in response to consumer demand. 'Career' then becomes a more general term denoting a pathway through life, rather than paid work or a job. Others state that such claims are exaggerated (Noon and Blyton 2007). Demographics indicate that fewer young people will enter the labour market in the next decade and concerns about the viability of pensions may mean that older people are likely to be forced to work longer and retire later. The future seems uncertain when the only constant is change.

What do young people understand by the term 'career'?

Many CLD practitioners working with young people report that the words 'career' and 'money' are seen to go hand in hand, with money being the major motivator for many young people. This is far removed from the wider notion of a pathway through life discussed in the previous section as notions of career as paid work to facilitate a comfortable and enjoyable life endure in the minds of many.

Contemporary definitions emphasise that career is about:

- inclusion – everyone has a career, it is part of their life as a whole;
- participation – engaging with society and contributing to the well-being of others through the work that they do;
- lifelong progression – making progress in learning and work throughout their lives;
- self-constructed identity – building and managing a positive identity and future for themselves;
- well-being – pursuing career happiness through the achievement of meaningful work.

Box 1.1 offers some definitions of 'career' by recent commentators.

Box 1.1 Definitions of career

The sequence and combination of roles that a person plays during the course of a lifetime.

(Super 1990)

The pattern of work-related experience that spans the course of a person's life.

(Greenhaus and Callanan 1994)

A person's engagement with society through involvement in the organisation of work.

(Collin and Young 2000)

Careers are, to a certain extent, a 'property' of organisations, and managed by them as part of HRM.

(Baruch 2004)

For many young people the word 'career' also continues to relate closely to what they will do when they leave school or full-time education. Over the last two decades, this particular transition has become prolonged (Roberts 1997), with many young people staying in education and training longer by remaining at school, entering government training schemes and/or going to further education or higher education. This trend is set to continue, with the raising of the participation age to 18 by 2015. In the future, we might expect career transitions of young people into adulthood to be prolonged even further, as many take longer to reach the point of financial independence (Furlong and Cartmell 2007).

Teenagers can be forgiven for their apparent obsession with the 'economic' dimension of career, as in the short term they begin to grapple with the complexities of thinking about their futures. Later on, many of them begin to realise that other dimensions of career are important too, such as the importance of how they feel about what they are doing, feeling valued as well as other aspects of their well-being and future happiness. All these form important facets of their career narrative, which they will write throughout their life course (see Chapter 11).

What makes the concept of career difficult for young people?

When talking with young people, it is clear that many of them find the concept of career difficult and there are a number of reasons for this:

- Most young people have little experience of the world of work. In the past, when young people were able to gain part-time work from the age of about 14, this gave many of them valuable work and life experiences on which to draw when the time came to think about careers. Now, relatively few employers will employ young people in any kind of paid work until they have taken their GCSE examinations. This limits the amount and type of experience that young people can gain to such things as paper rounds and a couple of weeks of work experience while at school. Without experience it is difficult to make decisions about the future, as the perennial question of 'How can I know if I want to do something before I have actually tried it' remains unanswered.

- For most young people the concept of career is abstract and one they can only imagine. Neuroscience teaches us that the human brain develops over many years, normally reaching full maturation by the early twenties. Contrary to popular myth, the brain also continues to develop over decades during adulthood (Blakemore and Frith 2005). During adolescence and the subsequent latter years of development, the brain increases its capacity for abstract thought, and some of the last areas to develop are the brain's capacity to evaluate in the abstract ('What happens if . . .'). Many young people are faced with questions related to making career decisions that require them to do this, when some will simply not be ready. For example, 'What happens if I fail my GCSEs?' 'What happens if I go to university, what will I do then?' However, we do not have the luxury of being able to say to young people; 'Why not leave making your career decisions until your brain is fully developed' and, equally, we are not sure either that this would go down too well with many of them if we did! Our education and training system demands that young people make choices, but for many their capacity for evaluative abstract thought will lag behind the kinds of decisions they have to make. It seems fair to assume then that all young people will need some support in this.

- Coleman and Hendry's (1999) focal theory of adolescence gives us some invaluable insights into how teenagers think, feel and behave. Having studied normal adolescent development for more than twenty years, they observed that young people develop attitudes and opinions about a range of relationships, and through this process develop their own identity. During adolescence, teenagers are faced with a wide range of transitions (e.g. physical, mental and emotional), yet most appear to cope well. Their research concludes that 'they cope by dealing with one issue at a time' (Coleman and Hendry 1999: 15) as it comes into focus for each individual. In this way, teenagers spread the process of change over a number of years, and gradually over time adapt to their changing circumstances. In relation to CLD, this gives valuable insights regarding the ways in which young people think about career and it would suggest that young people will be able to make most progress in their thinking when the whole area of career is in focus for them. It is also clear that the timing of this thinking will vary for different young people, and that perhaps the CLD process is likely to be most successful when it is led by them.

- Some aspects of youth culture and media misrepresent career by reinforcing stereotypes, glamorising certain occupations and suggesting on reality TV shows that career success can be instant. Peer group pressure can also deter some young people from envisaging and planning career for themselves (Foskett *et al.* 2003).

The continuing relevance of established theories and models

In this section we give an overview of established theories and models, exploring their enduring relevance to those involved in CLD today. The section is designed to offer you an overview of relevant approaches and to act as a signpost for those who want to explore this further. If this applies to you, we suggest that you read the chapter on career development theory in Gothard *et al.* (2001) and Killeen's (1996) chapter on career theory as starters. Both of these contain more detail regarding the approaches covered here.

Trait and factor matching approaches

Over the years, the ways in which people make their career choices have been the subject of much study and lively debate. Some of the earliest traces of CLD theory are found in the US in the work of Parsons (1909), who can be seen as the founder of vocational psychology. Parsons was an advocate for young people, women and the socially disadvantaged (O'Brien 2001) and the roots of CLD can be seen in the desires of certain individuals to help socially disadvantaged people to find a way forward through their circumstances. Parsons advocated that people need to understand themselves clearly (e.g. aptitudes, abilities, interests), have knowledge of work and what it requires, and have the ability to put these two things together through reasoning. This was the birth of what was later to be called trait and factor matching approaches (often referred to as person-environment fit approaches), and signalled the advent of career assessment and testing, which sought to match the individual with the job. This approach had some validity when people entered an occupation or trade and stayed within it for the majority (if not the whole) of their working lives, making progress up a hierarchical ladder of opportunities. The emphasis within trait and factor approaches is on individual differences; people are different, jobs are different and the two can be matched.

As the twentieth century progressed, other theorists took these ideas forward and the work of Rodger (1952) and his seven-point plan became very influential in the UK. In the US, Holland's (1985) theory of occupational personalities became particularly prominent. This is still very much in evidence today and there are a number of websites dedicated to helping people undertake online tests in order to assess their vocational preferences (Psychological Assessment Resources 2001).

Even though the origins of the trait factor approach are almost a hundred years old, many argue that it is far from being outdated or irrelevant. As time has progressed, matching approaches have become more sophisticated and the control has shifted from the expert doing the matching to individuals doing it for themselves. Such approaches still have an important place today, and can be particularly helpful to people who are facing some kind of turning point in their lives (such as curriculum choice, or leaving school). Examples of these approaches are ICT packages such as FastTomato, Kudos and PathfinderLive, where young people answer a range of questions about their interests and abilities and the program suggests a list of possible careers.

The strengths of trait and factor matching approaches lie in their capacity to give individuals a picture of themselves and to generate ideas regarding possible options for the future. This can often be helpful if the person has few ideas or is finding it difficult to think ahead. This can happen for a range of reasons (e.g. difficulties at home or at school, lack of motivation or low levels of self-esteem), and as people involved in CLD, it is important to remember that many young people will find using one of these programs helpful as part of the difficult process of thinking about their future. However, it is essential to understand that such approaches can often only give a snapshot in time. One danger is that they can promote a directive approach, where particular occupations are recommended in line with test results and young people can then slip into the trap of seeing them as prescriptive. Matching itself is useful, but is no substitute for the knowledge young people can gain about themselves and about career through experience.

Not forgetting DOTS

In relation to CLD, the DOTS model devised by Law and Watts (1977) for many years represented a significant explanation of the vital elements of the career education and guidance process. A summary of the model is set out below.

D	Decision learning	Understanding the different ways in which we make decisions. This often focuses on making informed choices.
O	Opportunity awareness	Researching and exploring options available (jobs, courses, careers). Use and evaluate information sources, including the internet to find career information, company information, and jobs.
T	Transition learning	Coping with and preparing for change (e.g. entry into the job market, further or higher education).
S	Self-awareness	Gaining an understanding of myself – my strengths and weaknesses, skills, interests and the things that will be important to me in a career.

Until 1995 this model was used by many people involved in CLD to help them devise programmes of careers education and guidance in schools, colleges, universities and other settings. It was often seen as a process of assessing myself (S), finding out about opportunities open to me (O), choosing which path to follow (D) and preparing for change (T).

Since 1995, the model developed by SCAA (1995) has dominated in the 11–19 sector, which is summarised as follows.

- Self-development – understanding ourselves and the influences upon us.
- Career exploration – investigating opportunities in learning and work.
- Career management – making and adjusting plans to manage change and transition.

The DOTS model still dominates in higher education, but even in this context McCash (2006) has questioned its position, arguing that the model has achieved a position of power that has stopped people challenging its relevance for twenty-first century society. This, he argues, has delayed the introduction of more innovative approaches and frameworks more closely suited to the career needs of young people and adults today.

During the 1990s, Law sought to move the DOTS model forward and developed a career-learning theory. Using verbs instead of nouns, he devised the SESIFU (Sensing, Sifting, Focusing and Understanding) model, which describes a learning process that people undertake in order to move their thinking forward in relation to their future. Building on his earlier community interaction theory (1981), Law asserts that people learn about career by drawing on a range of different sources within their community (including parents, teachers, employers, etc.) and points to the potential of positive role models and mentors for young people.

Developmental approaches

By the 1950s, the work of Super (1957) was becoming well known and he argued that people change and develop over time and with experience. Their views of themselves (or their self-concept) also change as they move towards maturity. Also, people can be seen to develop career patterns through their lives that result from their personality, the individual's socio-economic level (and that of their parents in the case of young people), and the opportunities to which they are exposed. Individuals, according to Super, can be seen to develop through the following five life stages.

- Growth – birth to 14 (including Fantasy 4–10, Interest 11–12 and Capacity 13–14)
- Exploration – 15–24, (including Tentative 15–17, Transition 18–21, and Trial 21–24)
- Establishment – 24–44, (including Trial 24–30, Stabilisation 31–44)
- Maintenance (44–64)
- Decline (65+).

Developmental approaches place an emphasis on the individual and can be helpful in seeking to gain some kind of lifelong picture of how individuals progress in their thinking about career and the different roles that people may have during their lifespan. But when considering the changing nature of career, work and society, perhaps we need to question the detail of the stages and roles outlined above. As people involved in CLD with young people, it would be a mistake to assume that the decisions of all 15 year olds are tentative. Some young people will be clear about the way forward for them and will already be engaged in thinking about their transition from education post-16. Others will need longer (some much longer) for this development to take place in their thinking. Any theory that appears to categorise people into ages and stages is open to question, as exceptions will always quickly emerge. Super's work has also faced criticism on the grounds of being male and middle-class orientated, and the term 'decline' does not describe the career experiences of older people very positively.

Developmental approaches emphasise the ways in which an individual's career develops over time throughout the life course and Super's (1981) rainbow model also shows the ways in which individuals take on different roles (e.g. student, worker, parent) and how these roles interact with one another. In his later 'archway' model, Super (1990) also considers the impact of society on individuals on the right-hand side of the arch, with the individual factors on the left. Both of these models provide a more holistic description of career, where work and other aspects of life are viewed alongside one another.

When thinking about developmental approaches, it is also important to consider other elements that can have an impact on an individual's career and their decision-making processes. These are as follows.

- *The locus of control.* When reading literature on motivation theory, the locus of control (Rotter 1966) is often highlighted as a key aspect that affects an individual's capacity to make decisions about their lives. Some individuals feel in charge of themselves and see themselves as agents of their own destiny. They are described as having a strong internal locus of control. Others feel that they have very little control over what happens to them, and are described as having a strong external locus of control. Lease (2004), in her study of university students, highlights that a strong external locus of control is associated with career decision-making difficulties.

When thinking about young people and their career motivations (as discussed previously), many can be seen to be motivated by money (external locus of control). However, this often changes over time, and many then begin to consider internal issues, such as job satisfaction and doing things that will enhance their sense of self-worth.

- *The importance of self-efficacy and self-management.* Bandura (1986) describes self-efficacy beliefs as an individual's judgement of their ability to carry out actions in order to reach their goals. Those with a high degree of self-efficacy believe that they are capable of organising themselves in order to carry out actions to achieve their goals. Kidd (2006) argues that it is important for those involved in CLD to understand the sources of self-efficacy. These are previous successes, vicarious learning and modelling, low levels of anxiety and encouragement and support from others (Bandura 1997, cited in Kidd 2006). This gives pointers to those involved in CLD to the ways in which young people can develop self-efficacy in relation to their career, where support will be crucial in order to lower their levels of anxiety.
- *The development of the self-concept.* The self-concept is a broad term used to describe how an individual views themselves generally. It has many dimensions and a young person's thoughts about their career forms just one part of these and is closely linked with their sense of identity. The self-concept develops throughout life, and particularly in adolescence, as young people strive to find their identity and place within the world (Coleman and Hendry 1999).
- *Self-esteem.* The term 'self-esteem' describes the value that the individual places on themselves and their feelings of personal worth. Low self-esteem can be linked to issues of depression and anxiety (Rosenberg 1965). Like the self-concept, self-esteem also has many facets; for example, a young person may have a high level of self-esteem in one area (e.g. sport) and low levels in other areas (e.g. academic work). Like the locus of control, successful experiences can enhance a young person's self-esteem.

Opportunity structure approach

Until the 1970s, theories of CLD were dominated by psychological approaches where individuals and their aspirations, needs and wishes were paramount. Until this point, much of the CLD literature emanated from the US, and it seems fair to say that the individualistic nature of American society did much to keep the individual at centre stage in relation to CLD. In the late 1970s, Roberts (1977) challenged this in his opportunity structure approach to career, where he argued (and still argues today) that the structures of society (in particular the variables of class, race and gender) have a greater effect on career choice than the wishes of the individual. Over time, Roberts developed his ideas as he witnessed the prolonged transitions that young people experience between school and work. The work of Roberts poses questions around the extent to which an individual can have control over their future and the impact of societal factors on career.

The traditional approaches outlined above have set the stage for what Cohen *et al.* (2000) refer to as the determinist/voluntarist debate. Within this debate, the extent to which individuals are conditioned by their external circumstances or have the capacity to create their own environment is ongoing and hotly contested.

Newer theories and models

In this section, we will consider some of the newer approaches to CLD that have emerged more recently. Again the purpose here is to present you with an overview, with references for those of you who wish to read further.

The Canadian Blueprint Model

Canada's Blueprint for Life/Work Design was developed by Redekopp *et al.* in the late 1990s and is a national career management skills framework. It was developed from the North American blueprint and is a framework of career-learning competencies.

The Blueprint for Life/Work Designs consists of four main components:

1   The competencies that people require, from childhood to adulthood, to manage their life/work development effectively.
2   A comprehensive process for developing and redesigning programmes and products that will help people acquire the above competencies in schools, post-secondary institutions, training programmes, career centres and other settings in which career development interventions occur.
3   Appendices full of information that support effective career development programming (needs assessments, other skills classification systems, portfolios, practitioner standards and guidelines, and career resources).
4   A Quick Reference Guide designed to help users quickly and efficiently find and use what they need within the Blueprint. (Adapted from Hache *et al.* 2006.)

The competencies are listed under three broad headings:

*   personal management
*   learning and work exploration
*   life/work building.

Each of these is written in four levels. Unlike the North American blueprint, these levels are not related to age, as research in the development stage showed that this forced career practitioners to focus on the achievement of the particular students concerned, irrespective of their age.

The Canadian Blueprint Model is based on a constructivist approach to career, which is discussed in more detail in Chapter 11. It is becoming widely recognised as an excellent resource for a range of CLD professionals, and an influential model for preparing people for their future career. The Australian Blueprint was rolled out in 2008 and it is possible that the UK will follow suit in adapting and testing the Blueprint. The National Life/Work Centre has an excellent website giving a wealth of information on the Blueprint, and we encourage you to visit it to find out more (http://206.191.51.163/blueprint/home.cfm).

The CASVE decision-making cycle

The Cognitive Information Processing (CIP) approach of Peterson *et al.* (1996) is a model based on a symbol processing approach. It has become well known and is often referred to as CASVE (see overleaf). This model was initially devised for careers work in higher education and puts forward a protocol for career decision-making. It can be summarised as follows:

—	Communication	Identifying a gap – knowing that I need to make a decision.
—	Analysis	Understanding myself and my options, thinking about alternatives.
	Synthesis	Creating likely alternatives, working out what can be done to solve the problem.
	Valuing	Prioritising alternatives, e.g. choosing an occupation, job, subject or course.
	Execution	Devising strategies to implement my choice.

It is often depicted as points on a cycle, or, in effect, a spiral.

This cycle or spiral represents the middle tier of a pyramid of information-processing domains, where the base is made up of self-knowledge and occupational knowledge and the apex is termed the executive processing domain, which involves thinking about the decision-making processes.

In order to help staff who are involved in CLD, Peterson *et al.* (2002) also identify seven key activities that can be provided by those with CLD expertise. These will help people engage with the cycle and are as follows.

1   Screen individuals for their readiness to make career decisions. As a minimum, this would involve asking people why they are seeking help and what they need. More sophisticated approaches could include asking people to complete some kind of self-assessment inventory.
2   Match levels of staff assistance to the needs of the individual. There are three levels identified: self-help (for those who have a high level of readiness), brief staff-assisted services (for those who have a moderate level of readiness) and individual case-managed services (for those with a low level of readiness).
3   Use career theory to help individuals understand and manage career decision-making. This helps students to understand the content of decisions (i.e. what they need to decide) and the process of decision-making (i.e. how they will decide).
4   Use the career resource room and internet websites with all levels of service delivery. Provide resources that are easy to use with indexes and guides to help people find the material they need. The resource room can be used unaided by some and with help by others.
5   Use career resources that are appropriate for diverse individual needs. Examine materials carefully to make sure that they cater for a range of needs and do not exclude large numbers of people.
6   Use staff teamwork to deliver services to individuals. If there is more than one member of staff delivering services, they need to work together in the interests of the student. Some individuals will prefer to work with one particular member of staff, others will be happy to work with more than one.
7   Provide common staff training for delivering resources and services. This ensures that service delivery is consistent.

The seven points above can form useful guidelines for those who are designing and delivering CLD activities in a range of settings.

Mitchell and Krumboltz's Social Learning Theory

In their early work on career decision-making, Mitchell *et al.* (1979) argued that both genetic endowment (e.g. race, gender and intelligence) and the environment (e.g. family, circumstances) influence the ways in which people make decisions. Based on the work of Bandura (1969), they assert that people learn through the following major types of learning experiences.

* *Instrumental* – learning that results from direct experience, when an individual is positively or negatively reinforced for their action.
* *Associative* – learning that involves the association of a previously neutral stimulus or experience with one that is laden with positive or negative associations. Such experiences can be either vicarious (indirect) or direct. Associative learning experiences help to account for the reasons why individuals come to feel positively or negatively toward certain occupations or work-related activities.

In their later work, Mitchell and Krumboltz (1996) developed their ideas further to provide a guide for career choice and counselling. They identify a role for CLD professionals in opening up experiences to their students, so that the students do not make their decisions based solely on their previous experiences. This provides a strong rationale for programmes of work experience and their relationship with promoting equality of opportunity.

The work of Hodkinson and his associates

During the 1990s, the work of Hodkinson and his associates has been influential in furthering the debate around the influences of society and culture on career choice. From their study of young people taking part in the Training Credits scheme, Hodkinson *et al.* (1996) developed their theory of career decision-making, entitled 'careership'. The concept of 'careership' has the following three dimensions:

* *Choices of lifestyle* – people always make decisions from within their social settings (what Bordieu, 1977, cited in Hodkinson *et al.* 1996 refers to as their habitus).
* *Individual progression over time* – circumstances change and people will often make decisions in response to these changing circumstances.
* *Social interactions with others* – these form an important part of the process as decisions are made in a social context.

Hodkinson *et al.* use the term 'pragmatic rationality' to describe the decision-making processes of the young people studied and it is markedly different from previous models of decision-making. They observed that the young people made their decisions in response to their circumstances and in line with what they call their 'horizons for action'. These were formed by notions that the young people had about themselves combined with knowledge of the opportunities around them, and their perceptions from their life histories regarding what they felt they could achieve. These 'horizons for action' are determined in part by an individual's cultural capital (Olneck 2000); for example, their successes in the education system and their values and their feelings of self-worth. Generally their findings suggest that, overall, society is a more dominant influence than the individual in relation to career choice, as in the majority of cases the young people they studied responded to their circumstances in a pragmatic way. In most cases, these actions tended to force the young people to conform to the norms of society.

It is clear from our consideration of newer approaches that the determinist/voluntarist debate continues and writers remain divided on how far individuals have control over their future, and the impact of societal factors on career choice and development. In Chapter 11 we consider the importance of new and emerging approaches that seek to take forward our understandings of career and the ways in which people make their choices.

Why bother with theory?

One of the hallmarks of any profession is that it has a body of relevant professional knowledge on which its members draw (Schön 1995). Aspects of this body of knowledge have been discussed in this chapter, and when reading it, you may have been tempted to think that it represents little more than common sense. In the area of CLD, it is a mistake to reduce this relevant professional knowledge to common sense available to anyone who can think and relate well to young people: this is simply not the case. Kurt Lewin once famously wrote 'there is nothing as practical as a good theory' (1951: 169) and theory is needed in order to help us gain insights into what we are doing and why. The world of CLD is no exception to this, particularly if it is to be taken seriously from a professional point of view.

In any professional area involving work with people, it is highly unlikely that one single theory or model will provide us with all we need to know. People do not come in standard sizes or packages, where a 'one size fits all' approach can work, but come with infinite variety. As a result, it is right to expect that any CLD professional will need to draw on a wide range of theory in order to inform their practice. CLD practice, like any other professional area, continues to develop and move forward, and in this respect new approaches will continue to be needed as our knowledge and understanding develop. Otherwise the whole area of CLD will stagnate and become irrelevant to today's young people. Some of these new approaches will be examined in Chapter 11.

Conclusion

In this chapter we have examined a wide range of literature that has informed our understanding of career over a long period of time. The amount and range of literature about career is vast and this chapter has given you an introduction to some of the key concepts that underpin CLD. Theory is important in helping us to understand how and why young people make their career decisions. Such understanding helps in the design and delivery of effective CLD, which eases and enhances this process. It is, of course, vital that theory keeps up with the pace of change in the globalised world and research plays a key part in this process and is the focus of the next chapter.

Discussion points

1 Discuss with some young people who you have contact with what they understand by the word 'career'.
2 How easy or difficult do they find it to think about it and why?
3 Think about the traditional approaches outlined. How far do you feel they apply to the young people you are working with?
4 Are the newer approaches more relevant?
5 Do you think an understanding of theory is important to your work in CLD? Think about your reasons.

References

Bandura, A. (1969) *Principles of Behaviour Modification*, New York: Rinehart and Winston.

Bandura, A. (1986) *Social Foundations of Thought and Action: a Social Cognitive Theory*, Englewood Cliffs, NJ: Prentice Hall.

Baruch, Y. (2004) *Managing Careers: Theory and Practice*, Harlow: Prentice Hall.

Blakemore, S.-J. and Frith, U. (2005) *The Learning Brain, Lessons for Education*, Oxford: Blackwell Publishing.

Cohen, L., Manion, L. and Morrison, K. (2000) *Research Methods in Education*, 5th edn, London: Routledge.

Coleman, J.C. and Hendry, L.B. (1999) *The Nature of Adolescence*, 3rd edn, London: Routledge.

Collin, A. and Young, R.A. (2000) *The Future of Career*, Cambridge: Cambridge University Press.

Edwards, R. (1993) 'The inevitable future? Post-Fordism in work and learning' in R. Edwards, S. Sieminski and D. Zeldin (eds.) *Adult Learners, Education and Training*, London: Routledge.

Foskett, N., Lumby, J. and Maringe, F. (2003) Pathways and progression at 16+ – 'fashion', peer influence and college choice. Paper presented to the Annual Conference of the British Educational Research Association, Heriot-Watt University, Edinburgh, 11–13 September. Online: www.leeds. ac.uk/educol/documents/00003252.doc (accessed 13 February 2010).

Furlong, A. and Cartmell, F. (2007) *Young People and Social Change*, Maidenhead: McGraw-Hill.

Gothard, B., Mignot, P., Offer, M. and Ruff, M. (2001) *Careers Guidance in Context*, London: Sage.

Greenhaus, J.H. and Callanan, G.A. (1994) *Career Management*, Fort Worth: The Dryden Press.

Hache, L., Redekopp, D.E and Jarvis, P.S. (2006) *Blueprint for Life/Work Designs The Quick Reference Guide*, Canada, National Life/Work Centre.

Hodkinson, P., Sparkes, A.C. and Hodkinson, H. (1996) *Triumphs and Tears: Young People, Markets and the Transition from School to Work*, London: David Fulton Publishers.

Holland, J. (1985) *Making Vocational Choices: a Theory of Vocational Personalities and Work Environments*, 2nd edn, Englewood Cliffs, NJ: Prentice-Hall.

Kidd, J.M. (2006) *Understanding Career Counselling: Theory, Research and Practice*, London: Sage.

Killeen, J. (1996) 'Career theory' in A.G. Watts, J. Killeen, J.M. Kidd and R. Hawthorne (eds.) *Rethinking Careers Education and Guidance: Theory, Policy and Practice*, London: Routledge.

Law, B. (1981) 'Community interaction: a mid-range focus for theories of career development in young adults', *British Journal of Guidance and Counselling*, 9: 142–158.

Law, B. and Watts, A.G. (1977) *Schools, Careers and Community*, London: Church Information Office.

Lease, S. (2004) 'Effect of locus of control, work knowledge and mentoring on career decision-making difficulties: testing the role of race and academic institution', *Journal of Career Assessment*, 12: 239–254.

Lewin, K. (1951) *Field Theory in Social Science*, Chicago, University of Chicago.

McCash, P. (2006) 'We're all career researchers now: breaking open career education and DOTS', *British Journal of Guidance and Counselling*, 34: 429–449.

Mitchell, A., Jones, G. and Krumboltz, J. (1979) *Social Learning and Career Decision Making*, Rhode Island: Carroll.

Mitchell, L.K. and Krumboltz, J.D. (1996) 'Krumboltz's learning theory of career choice and counseling', in D. Brown, L. Brooks and Associates (eds.) *Career Choice and Development*, 3rd edn, San Francisco, CA: Jossey Bass.

Noon, M. and Blyton, P. (2007) *The Realities of Work: Experiencing Work and Employment in Contemporary Society*, Houndmills, Basingstoke and Hampshire, NY: Palgrave.

O'Brien, K.M. (2001) 'The legacy of Parsons: career counselors and vocational psychologists as agents of social change', *Career Development Quarterly*, 50: 66–76.

Olneck, M. (2000) 'Can multicultural education change what counts as cultural capital?', *American Educational Research Journal*, 37: 317–348.

Parsons, F. (1909) *Choosing a Vocation*, Boston: Houghton Mifflin.

Peterson, G.W., Sampson, J.P., Jr., Lenz, J.G. and Reardon, R.C. (2002) 'A cognitive information processing approach to career problem solving and decision making', in D. Brown (ed.) *Career Choice and Development*, 4th edn, San Francisco, CA: Jossey-Bass.

Peterson, G.W., Sampson, J.P.S. Jr., Reardon, R.C. and Lenz, J.G. (1996) 'A cognitive information processing approach to career problem solving and decision making', in D. Brown, L. Brooks and Associates (eds.) *Career Choice and Development*, 3rd edn, San Francisco, CA: Jossey Bass.

Psychological Assessment Resources (2001) Welcome to the Self Directed Search by John Holland. Online: www.self-directed-search.com (accessed 29 January 2010).

Roberts, K. (1977) 'The social conditions, consequences and limitations of careers guidance', *British Journal of Guidance and Counselling*, 5: 1–9.

Roberts, K. (1997) 'Prolonged transitions to uncertain destinations', *British Journal of Guidance and Counselling*, 25: 345–360.

Roberts, K. (2005) 'Social class, opportunity structures and career guidance' in B. Irving, and B. Malik (eds.) *Critical Reflections on Career Education and Guidance: Promoting Social Justice within a Global Economy*, London: RoutledgeFalmer.

Rodger, A. (1952) *The Seven Point Plan*, National Institute of Industrial Psychology.

Rosenberg, M. (1965) *Society and the Adolescent Self-image*, Princeton: Princeton University Press.

Rotter, J.B. (1966) 'Generalized expectancies for internal versus external control of reinforcement', *Psychological Monographs*, 80 (1) (Whole No. 609).

SCAA (1995) *Looking Forward*, London: SCAA.

Schön, D. (1995) *Reflective Practitioner: How Professionals Think in Action*, Aldershot: Arena.

Storey, J.A. (2000) 'Fracture lines in the career environment' in A. Collin and R.A. Young (eds.) *The Future of Career*, Cambridge: Cambridge University Press.

Super, D.E. (1957) *The Psychology of Careers*, New York: Harper Row.

Super, D.E. (1981) 'A developmental theory', in D. Montrose and C. Shinkman (eds.) *Career Development in the 1980s*, Springfield, MA: Montrose.

Super, D.E. (1990) 'A life-span approach to career development', in D. Brown and L. Brooks (eds.) *Career Choice and Development*, 2nd edn, SanFrancisco: Jossey-Bass.

Unwin, L. and Wellington, J. (2001) *Young People's Perspectives on Education, Training and Employment: Realizing their Potential*, London: Kogan Page.

Walker, I. and Zhu, Y. (2005) *The College Wage Premium, Overeducation, and the Expansion of Higher Education in the UK*, Bonn: Institute for the Study of Labor.

Chapter 2

Research perspectives

The purpose of developmental CLD research is to investigate planned changes to find out what is happening, what works and how to proceed. By way of contrast, evaluative research is concerned with assessing the value or worth of particular CLD provision and activities.

Typically, what researchers do is to create a hypothesis, review the existing literature that can help with their research, choose a methodology for testing their hypothesis that is 'fit for purpose', implement their research, analyse and interpret their findings and present their report. Great variation of approach occurs within the research process. For example, research can be small or large scale, single or mixed method, practitioner led or researcher led, robust or flawed, and badly disseminated or well disseminated! Many useful resources exist to guide student researchers through the process of conducting their own research projects (e.g. Bell 2005; Burton *et al.* 2008).

Engaging with CLD research

If you have ever wondered why you are reluctant to read research reports, look no further than your interest type. Practitioners (teachers, advisers, etc.) usually score highly on the 'social' scale according to Holland's (1997) theory of person–environment fit, whereas researchers are 'investigative' types. This is not, of course, an excuse for ignoring CLD research; and any difficulties you may have with engaging with careers research may have other causes such as lack of time or, to lay some of the responsibility at the feet of researchers themselves, their failure to make their findings accessible to practitioners. Why is it important that we engage with CLD research? A number of compelling arguments can be advanced:

- Research is a way of finding out what is important and what works in career learning and development – i.e. is this worth doing?
- The insights provided by research can help us to improve our effectiveness – i.e. what should we do next?
- Research poses new questions that will enable us to change and develop our practice – i.e. what works well and what could we do better?
- Research helps us to test out the career theories to which we, explicitly or implicitly, subscribe – i.e. how does theory help?
- Research helps us to check out the accuracy of trends and developments that have been predicted or identified – i.e. am I right when I say . . .?
- Practice raises questions which can only be answered through carefully constructed research – i.e. why isn't what I'm doing working?

Once you have decided to engage with research, the question is: 'How will you do so?' Your school may already be actively engaged in research (NFER, for example, runs an award scheme for research-engaged schools). You may be invited to participate in an external research project – in which case you may need to weigh up the pros and cons of taking part. On the positive side, you will be contributing to the development of CLD and will gain useful insights into the school's own provision. However, you need to be clear about the likely demands on yourself, staff and students.

Undertaking your own small-scale research is another way of getting involved. Action research is a methodology that lends itself to school-led research (we discuss this in Chapter 9).

Perhaps the most common way of engaging with research is as a 'critical consumer'. To do this, you will need to be able to:

- spot the limitations or flaws in a research report either unaided or with the help of a research review;
- make decisions about the applicability of the findings to the situation in which you work;
- recognise that terms such as 'some of the schools in the study', 'our findings suggest', 'perceived to make a difference' and 'found an association' mean what they say, neither more nor less.

Training yourself to become a critical consumer of research involves a permanent change in the way in which you carry out your role. You will need to build into your routines a regular mechanism for keeping abreast of relevant research in your sector. Box 2.1 suggests ways of keeping abreast of new research.

Box 2.1 Ways of finding out about careers research

Through support networks:

- Your local Connexions service

Through subject and professional associations (e.g. their websites, journals and conferences):

- Association for Careers Education and Guidance – www.aceg.org.uk
- Institute of Career Guidance – www.icg-uk.org. ICG members can use the iCeGS research enquiry service using the form available at www.derby.ac.uk/Ask_iCeGS
- International Association for Educational and Vocational Guidance (IAEVG) – www.iaevg.org/IAEVG/.

Through centres/organisations involved in career research and development:

- Centre for Career and Personal Development, CCCU – www.canterbury.ac.uk/education/career-and-personal-development/Home.aspx

- International Centre for Guidance Studies – www.derby.ac.uk/iCeGS
- National Foundation for Educational Research – www.nfer.ac.uk, e.g. on the web (www.nfer.ac.uk/ontheweb/)
- National Guidance Research Forum website contains research, practice and training materials to support practitioners, trainers, managers and policy-makers –www.guidance-research.org/
- National Institute for Careers Education and Counselling – www.nicec.org.uk.

Through general education sources:

- DfE and DCSF research (www.education.gov.uk/research/)

Through researcher social network sites:

Citeulike (www.citeulike.org/) is a social networking referencing tool which you can use to maintain your own reference library and link to other useful resources such as the iCeGS library (www.citeulike.org/user/iCeGS).

You may also find it useful to design and use a 'research digest' template for recording key information about research studies that are relevant to your work. A completed example is shown in Box 2.2.

Box 2.2 Research Digest template

Full reference: author(s), year, title, place of publication, publisher
Stoney, S., Ashby, P., Golden, S. and Lines, A. (1998) *Talking about 'Careers': Young People's Views of Careers Education and Guidance at School* (RD 18). Sheffield: DfEE.

Location (web address if accessed online, file and folder name if stored on own computer, file or shelf reference if printed copy stored)

Overview
Group discussions with Y11 and post-16 students about how they felt about the CEG they'd received.

Main findings
- Most had not experienced a careers programme. They were aware of scattered activities and were confused about the roles of staff. They felt CEG lacked status and was tainted by its association with PSE.
- Self-awareness activities – they often did not like, or feel confident in, discussing themselves in front of others. They could not see how this linked in with making career choices. They commented on the strange job suggestions on computer-print-outs.
- Careers information – they were concerned that information was restricted, partial, sometimes out of date, unattractive, inaccessible (too much writing). Too many problems with using IT to research careers information for themselves.

- The guidance interview – mixed comments. Worked best when adviser was known, trusted, a good listener and responsive. Was worst when students were poorly prepared and adviser unknown to them and unresponsive.
- Out-of-school learning – they really valued first-hand experience, e.g. work experience, open days, careers conventions, visits and visitors.
- Delivery mechanisms – Need to make it more coherent and continuous, start earlier (don't leave it all to Y11), improve the timing of elements and make it more differentiated (e.g. small-group work), help build trusting relationships with advisers, less information giving and more practical and active learning.
- Conclusions – much unfilled potential in current CEG provision. Listen to the clients more.

Additional notes
Includes the schedules used for the focus group discussions.

Action points
Do our own consultation exercise.

Literature reviews

Literature reviews are particularly helpful for weighing up the balance of evidence about the effectiveness and impact of CLD, and raising issues and challenges for policy, research and practice. Reviewers are often quite cautious and circumspect about the conclusions they draw especially in the light of gaps and shortcomings in the research evidence. The headlines from some key reviews, including two from outside the English secondary sector, are summarised in Box 2.3.

Box 2.3 Literature reviews

Bowes, L., Smith, D. and Morgan, S. (2005). *Reviewing the Evidence Base for Careers Work in Schools*. Derby: Centre for Guidance Studies, University of Derby.

- Considered twenty studies published after 1988 of CEG and the transition process at KS3 and KS4. It looked at effectiveness, inhibitors and the influence that other external and internal factors can have on young people's perceptions and experiences of transitions.
- Evidence suggested that 'a good-quality careers education programme, coupled with impartial guidance provision, can equip pupils with the career-related skills they need in order to make informed decisions and successful transitions at KS3 and KS4, provided that they are tailored to individual rather than organisational needs, appropriately integrated into the timetable and the wider curriculum, and delivered at relevant points in time by suitably qualified staff.'

Hughes, D. and Gration, G. (2009). *Literature Review of Research on the Impact of Careers and Guidance-related Interventions*. Reading: CfBT Education Trust.

- Focused primarily on informing and consolidating professionals' understanding of what constitutes effective CEIAG-related interventions as well as identifying gaps in the evidence-base for measuring and assessing the impact of CEIAG provision in England.
- Over 100 studies reviewed and the key findings of forty-five of these studies included in the report.
- Conclusions presented under five headings. In relation to the impact of CEIAG interventions, the review concluded that 'the impact of CEIAG interventions in terms of participation and retention in education, training, employment and other "hard" outcomes is open to interpretation . . . However, there is a reasonably strong case to be made that CEIAG interventions can and do make a difference in terms of "soft" outcomes such as increased self-confidence and enhanced decision-making skills that can be seen as *pre-cursors or proxy indicators* that make a significant contribution to longer-term socio-economic outcomes.'

Morris, M. (2004) *The Case for Careers Education and Guidance for 14-19 year olds.* Slough: NFER. Online: www.cegnet.co.uk/files/CEGNET001/resources/483. doc (accessed 10 January 2010).

- Summarised ten years of research by NFER into CEG practice and outcomes.
- Identified the skills that promote successful transition and traced some of the links between successful transition and programmes of careers education and guidance.
- Concluded that, at present, findings from these various NFER studies suggest that neither schools nor Connexions Services are in a position to provide the extent and quality of careers education and guidance that is necessary to promote positive student transitions for all young people at 16.

LSIS (2009) *Career Leadership for the 21ˢᵗ Century: A Leadership Issue for the FE Sector.* Coventry: LSIS.

- Noted the paucity of recent published research in the Further Education sector into the impact of career learning, information, advice and guidance (CLIAG).
- Reported 'indicative findings of the benefits of effective CLIAG in supporting recruitment, retention, engagement, motivation, achievement and progression . . . There is a larger body of evidence indicating an association between effective CLIAG and retention, and the contribution of realistic taster experiences to making informed decisions.'

Hughes, K.L. and Karp, M.M. (2004) *School-Based Career Development: A Synthesis of the Literature.* New York: Columbia University, Institute on Education and the Economy Teachers College. Online: www.tc.columbia.edu/iee/PAPERS/Career_Development_2004.pdf (accessed 10 January 2010).

- Reviewed more than fifty studies of school-based guidance and career development.
- Reported the findings of a meta-analysis by Whiston, Sexton and Lasoff (1998) which found that career guidance interventions have a positive (though

moderate) effect. This analysis also found that interventions with the largest effect were those that focused on a specific career-related skill, rather than 'career preparation' generally.

- Concluded that researchers have found benefits to students of comprehensive guidance programmes, career courses, academic counselling and computer-based guidance systems. However, there were also limitations to the interventions, many of which were short-term, low-dosage activities with unclear lasting benefits: 'Students do seem to benefit, both vocationally and academically, from participation in career courses. In particular, they seem to increase their knowledge of careers and their ability to make career-related decisions. On most career-related measures, students did see increased outcomes when compared with students not enrolled on a career course. In the one study exploring academic measures (Fouad, 1995), participants on a career course did improve academically. However, there is little evidence that any gains – either academic or career-related – are maintained over time.'
- Reported that career development activities that were more experiential in nature were found to positively influence such variables as school attendance and completion.
- Found that career guidance and academic counselling was potentially very effective with middle school students (age 11–14).

Key areas of research

An inputs–processes–outcomes model provides a structured way of discussing key areas of research into CLD in schools:

- What is needed? The type and adequacy of inputs into CLD is a vital area of research. We need to know more about the impact of the timing of inputs as well as the amount of curriculum time required. Studies to clarify the benefits of starting CLD earlier in the primary school are also needed. Staffing inputs are another key area. We need to understand the pros and cons of different staffing arrangements and how best to develop staff for their CLD roles.
- What works? Schools need help with selecting types of interventions that have proven efficacy. General educational research as well as specific CLD research can illuminate the teaching and learning methods that are most effective (see Chapters 5 and 6). Research into the needs of specific groups (e.g. the gifted and talented, learners with difficulties and disabilities) can help with designing more appropriate provision and moving away from the 'one size fits all' approach. Studies that shed light on the interaction of different processes are particularly valuable such as 'How can we strengthen the interaction between formal and informal CLD processes?' 'How can we develop home–school links in relation to CLD?' and 'How do gender and ethnicity combine, and what are the implications for the CLD provision we make?'
- What's the impact? This type of research endeavours to show the outcomes of CLD for young people. Hughes (2002) has identified three types of impact study. Opinion studies provide a subjective measure of impact. They rely on systematic feedback from young people about their perceptions of the services they have received. They are

straightforward to conduct and are relatively easy for practitioners to attempt on a small scale. Controlled studies (i.e. with a treatment group and a control group) are more complex to undertake and less common in our field. This is partly because of the difficulty of overcoming the ethical concerns of not providing 'treatment' to the control group. The DCSF Key Stage 2 Career-related learning pathfinder project (2009–2010), for example, dealt with this by using pupils in schools outside the project as the control group rather than by withholding CLD activities to some of the pupils in the project schools. The pupils in the control group were, therefore, not deprived of the CLD activities that their schools normally provide. Outcome studies try to provide evidence of the results of CLD interventions. They are popular with stakeholders who are interested in accountability and return on investment, but the results of studies carried out so far show that even so-called objective outcomes are open to interpretation.

Impact of CLD interventions

In relation to CLD research, Hughes (2007) has identified three types of outcomes:

*   *Personal attribute outcomes* – for example, changes in attitudes, motivation, self-esteem which are pre-cursors or pre-conditions that affect the person's ability to achieve other types of outcome.
*   *Learning outcomes* – for example, personal development, career exploration and career management knowledge and skills that can be gained from specific interventions and opportunities.
*   *Impact outcomes* – for example, moving into a job or another progression outcome which brings practical social and economic benefits.

The first two types are often referred to as 'soft' outcomes and the third type is referred to as a 'hard' outcome of CLD.

Personal attribute outcomes

Factors such as a feelings of self-worth, internal 'locus of control', strong self-efficacy beliefs, positive attitudes, resilience and high motivation are strongly associated with benefiting from CLD programmes and achieving learning and impact outcomes. Landmarks in research into personal attribute outcomes include:

*   Stoney, S. *et al.* (1998) reported that young people with low self-image chose poorer progression options, choosing post-16 courses with qualifications at the same level (or even at a lower level) than those which they had already achieved.
*   Morris *et al.* (1999) reported that the key factor that seemed to underpin successful transition at 16 was the level of young people's career-exploration skills. In addition, those who were most positive about their post-16 destinations showed that they were self-aware and able to apply their self-awareness.
*   Morris and Rutt (2003) highlighted the importance of good careers education and guidance programmes on young people's aspirations and the development of positive attitudes to higher education.
*   Moynagh and Worsley (2005) reported that the proportion of employees seeing themselves as having a career increased from just under half to 60 per cent between

1985 and 2001. The evidence also revealed how young people 'appeared firmly wedded to careers'.

Learning outcomes

Learning outcomes describe what individuals should know, understand and be able to do in a particular context and to a specified level of performance. They are used in curriculum design (see Chapter 5) to inform the selection of suitable teaching, learning and assessment activities. Several different frameworks have been devised to identify desirable or worthwhile career learning outcomes from CLD provision (see Box 2.4).

Landmarks in research into learning outcomes include:

* Killeen, J. (1996) 'The learning and economic outcomes of guidance' in A.G. Watts *et al. Rethinking Careers Education and Guidance.* London: Routledge. Killeen concluded that 'Guidance can and does lead to learning outcomes and associated changes in individuals' (p. 78) but that more research was still needed in this area (p. 88).

Box 2.4 Learning outcome frameworks in CLD

England

Careers Education Framework 7–19 (DCSF 2010). This framework is a mix of different types of outcome statements. The statements are stage-related (i.e. KS2, KS3, KS4 and 16–19) and organised under the six principles of impartial careers education. It replaces *Careers Education and Guidance in England – A national framework 11–19* (DfES 2003).

Wales

The Welsh Assembly Government also replaced its previous framework in 2008. *Careers and the World of Work: a framework for 11 to 19-year-olds* (Department for Children, Education, Lifelong Learning and Skills) lists outcomes under five headings: personal achievement, seeking information, understanding the world of work, guidance, and making and implementing decisions.

Blueprint

The Blueprint for Life/Work Designs developed as a collaboration between Canadian and US partners (http://206.191.51.163/blueprint/home.cfm). It was adapted for use throughout Australia and launched in 2008 (www.blueprint.edu.au/index. php). Interest in adapting Blueprint for the UK is also growing (e.g. www.lsis.org. uk/Documents/Publications/CareerLearningBlueprintWeb.pdf).

Blueprint differs from the current frameworks in England and Wales in that it is an all-age framework with outcomes at four levels. It identifies eleven main competencies under three headings: personal management, learning and work exploration, and career building.

- DfEE (1998) *The Influence of Careers Education and Guidance upon Pupils in Year 11.* SWA Consulting used an ambitious research design involving questionnaires and interviews with 603 students in Y11 in five East Midlands careers service areas which yielded rich data. They found that pupils had already achieved a high level of learning outcomes by the start of Year 11, leading to significant progress in only a few areas such as decision-making and decidedness during Year 11. They concluded that earlier career inputs may be more significant for end of Year 11 outcomes than inputs received during Year 11.

Impact outcomes

Research into the impact of CLD interventions on participation and retention in education, training and employment is extensive. Evidence linking CLD interventions to improvements in academic attainment are mixed but there is an association with improvements in retention in full-time education and reduced course-switching (Hughes and Gration 2009).

Impact outcomes are of particular interest to young people and their parents and carers. They are of even more interest to policy-makers and funders who often load high expectations onto CEIAG and require evidence of a 'return on investment'. At different times, for example, CEIAG has been expected to play a key role as a panacea for problems such as youth unemployment, preparing young people for employment, raising aspirations, improving retention and achievement, challenging stereotyping, combating social exclusion and promoting social inclusion. One of the research difficulties is in separating the impact of CEIAG from the other variables that have a bearing on solutions to these problems. Indeed, it is possible that CEIAG is most effective in combination with other strategies and that what is needed is further research to elucidate this.

The use of some impact measures also raises the issue of whether they are, strictly speaking, outcomes of CEIAG. A reduction in the numbers of those not in education, employment or training (NEET) may be a national issues to which CEIAG can contribute, but its solution lies in tackling a range of structural socio-economic problems as well. This is why researchers in the careers field are interested in the notion of 'distance travelled'. If we can demonstrate that a careers intervention has had a positive effect in moving a young person on from where they were before, then this could be evidence of 'value added'. Unfortunately, at the level of public policy-making, these effects are often regarded as 'intermediate' and carry little weight with decision-makers.

Landmarks in research into impact outcomes include:

- SWA Consulting (1999) found an association between low drop-out rates and those who had received specialist careers advice.
- Killeen *et al.* (1992) found evidence that guidance reduced the duration of job search and unemployment, but increased job retention and reduced floundering behaviour.
- Morris *et al.* (2000) reported evidence in one case-study school of the impact of a comprehensive careers education and guidance programme, introduced in the mid-1990s, on student outcomes. This pointed to improved GCSE results, the virtual elimination of switching and drop-out from post-16 study and minimal drop-out from higher education.
- The Transitions Review Group (EPPI 2004) concluded that 'there is also evidence that appropriate and relevant CEG can, and does, impact upon the transitions made by young people at the age of 16' (p. 9).

Conclusion

We have looked at some of the practical ways in which we can use the results of research to improve our practice. From the research base, it is clear that there are still considerable gaps in our understanding of what is needed, what works and what the impact is of CLD provision. We will always discover new areas where research is needed so where will the research centres be and where will the funding come from to carry out much-needed research in the future? We can benefit a lot from international research evidence, but we are probably over-reliant on American research evidence. The lack of long-term studies is a problem as this kind of research is expensive. The DCSF and its predecessors have commissioned much of the research that has been discussed in this chapter in support of their policy initiatives; and various charitable trusts have also been generous with their support, but it has been more difficult for CLD to attract funding from major research bodies. Nevertheless, there are currently some interesting pockets of research into aspects such as career well-being, narrative approaches and life-design which we will consider in Part C, but now in Chapter 3 we will explore the impact of policy on everyday practice.

Discussion points

1   How can practitioners become research-aware and research-engaged?
2   How can we use the results of research in practical ways to improve the effectiveness of CLD?

References

Bell, J. (2005) *Doing Your Research Project,* 4th edn, Milton Keynes: Open University Press.

Bowes, L., Smith, D. and Morgan, S. (2005) *Reviewing the Evidence Base for Careers Work in Schools,* Derby: Centre for Guidance Studies, University of Derby. Online: www.derby.ac.uk/files/icegs_reviewing_the_evidence_base_for_careers_work_in_schools_2005.pdf (accessed 14 February 2010).

Burton, N., Brundrett, M. and Jones, M. (2008) *Doing your Education Research Project,* London: Sage.

DCELLS (2008) *Careers and the World of Work: a Framework for 11–19-year-olds in Wales,* Cardiff: Department for Children, Education, Lifelong Learning and Skills. Online: http://wales.gov.uk/dcells/graphics/images/dcells/curriculumandassessment/arevisedcurriculumforwales/careersandtheworldofwork/careersworldofworkframework/careersworldofworkframeworke.pdf;jsessionid=MRCfL1lTvJvjWCPg3Yj010HysBHn7Kl2twR2VR9bLF37QJTGdMTc!-1041720684?lang=en (accessed 14 February 2010)

DCSF (2010) *Careers Education Framework 7–19,* London: DCSF. Online: www.cegnet.co.uk/files/CEGNET0001/wayschoices/docs/Careers-education-framework-7–19.pdf (accessed 14 February 2010).

DfES (2003) *Careers Education and Guidance in England – A national framework 11–19,* Nottingham: DfES. Online: www.cegnet.co.uk/files/CEGNET0001/resources/651.pdf (accessed 14 February 2010).

EPPI (2004) *A Systematic Review of Research into the Impact of Careers Education and Guidance during Key Stage 4 on Young People's Transitions to Post-16 Opportunities,* London: EPPI-Centre. Online: http://eppi.ioe.ac.uk/EPPIWebContent/reel/review_groups/transitions/transitions_protocol2.pdf (accessed 14 February 2010).

Holland, J.L. (1997) *Making Vocational Choices,* Odessa, FL: Psychological Assessment Resources.

Hughes, D. (2007) 'Assessing the Impact of Careers Work', presentation to the ACEG Conference, 7 July.

Hughes, D. and Gration, G. (2009) *Literature Review of Research on the Impact of Careers and Guidance–related Interventions*, Reading: CfBT Education Trust. Online: www.cfbt.com/evidence-foreducation/pdf/E&I%20Synthesis_FINAL%28Web%29%20.pdf (accessed 14 February 2010).

Hughes, D., Bosley, S., Bowes, L. and Bysshe, S. (2002) *The Economic Benefits of Guidance*, Derby: Centre for Guidance Studies, University of Derby.

Killeen, J. (1996) 'The learning and economic outcomes of guidance' in A.G. Watts, B. Law, J. Killeen, J. Kidd and R. Hawthorn (eds.), *Rethinking Careers Education and Guidance*. London: Routledge.

Killeen, J., White, M. and Watts, A.G. (1992) *The Economic Value of Careers Guidance*, London: Policy Studies Institute.

Morris, M. (2004) The *Case for Careers Education and Guidance for 14-19 year olds*, Slough: NFER. Online: www.leeds.ac.uk/educol/documents/00003578.htm (accessed 13 February 2010).

Morris, M. and Rutt, S. (2003) *Aspirations to Higher Education: a Baseline Analysis*, DCSF. Online: www.dcsf.gov.uk/research/data/uploadfiles/rr651.pdf (accessed 13 February 2010).

Morris, M., Golden, S. and Lines, A. (1999) *The Impact of Careers Education and Guidance on Transition at 16*, Sheffield: DfEE.

Morris, M., Rudd, P., Nelson, J. and Davies, D. (2000) *The Contribution of Careers Education and Guidance to School Effectiveness in 'Partnership' Schools*, Research Brief 198–199. London: DfEE. Online: http://publications.dcsf.gov.uk/eOrderingDownload/RB198-99.pdf (accessed 14 February 2010).

Moynagh, M. and Worsley, R. (2005) *Working in the Twenty-first Century*, Leeds: Economic and Social Research Council.

Stoney, S., Ashby, P., Golden, S. and Lines, A. (1998) *Talking about 'Careers': Young People's Views of Careers Education and Guidance at School* (RD 18), Sheffield: DfEE.

SWA Consulting (1999) *Evaluation of Early Individual Learning Account Development Activity*, London: DfEE. Online: www.education.gov.uk/research/data/uploadfiles/RB123.pdf (accessed 14 February 2010).

Chapter 3

Policy perspectives

The influence and interaction of theory, research, policy and practice on CLD provision is complex and fascinating. In this chapter, we focus on the impact of government policy on the purpose and position of careers education, information, advice and guidance (CEIAG) in the education system. We consider how schools respond to policy initiatives and discuss why it is important that CLD professionals should be aware of the policy implications of what they do.

Not all CLD professionals take an interest in policy-making or want to influence policy agendas, but some do and need to do so if the profession is to win the hearts and minds of policy-makers and to secure continuing support for CLD provision. This also means being prepared to listen to what policy-makers expect of the careers profession.

The influence of policy on practice is often more direct than the influences of theory and research. Kidd *et al.* (1994), for example, found a consensus of approach among career guidance practitioners that they could locate in career theory, but that practitioners could not always do for themselves, but their practice reflected the policy of their service and their organisations. The expansion of the target-driven culture in public services in the 1990s has had its effect on career guidance staff whose work has been increasingly linked to funding and the achievement of policy targets.

Policy-making tied to evidence-based practice is often held up as the ideal, but this can be undermined when policy-makers cherry-pick evidence that justifies the positions they already hold. An example of this is when rather naïve statements are made about the use of ICT in CLD provision. Becta, the government agency that promoted the use of ICT in education, undertook a number of important projects in the 1990s that came to a halt after the publication of *Connecting Careers & ICT* (Becta 2001). Since then, research evidence on how to use ICT effectively in CLD practice has been slight. The policy of using ICT seems to be based on little more than the rationale that young people today are comfortable using ICT and using ICT will cut labour costs.

Another tendency of policy-makers in education is to prefer quantitative research to qualitative studies. It is easy to see the appeal of 'hard' data that shows how large numbers of young people have benefited from an intervention in order to justify the general direction of policy, but illuminative case studies are often more revealing and inspirational for improving CLD practice.

School outcomes from CLD policy-making

What do we know about the range of outcomes for schools from national CLD policy-making? Well-attested effects include the following.

Compliance

The first responsibility of governors and senior leaders is to ensure that they meet statutory requirements. Those relating to careers education in England are summarised in *A Guide to the Law for School Governors* updated periodically by the DCSF (2009a). The wider consequence of compliance is that policy shapes the type of CLD provision that schools make. The emphasis on 'choices and transitions' activities in school careers programmes, for example, can be related to government priorities on inclusion, participation, retention, progression and preparation for employability, but as Kidd (2006) has argued, preparation for career well-being and happiness is more important for young people in the longer term. What can careers professionals do to ensure that what is important is not driven out by what is urgent?

Leverage

Policy initiatives can be catalysts for change. Leaders of CLD will harness the policy implementation process to facilitate change in their own schools. The Year 9–10 initiative launched in 1994, for example, was largely successful in encouraging schools in England to strengthen careers work for 12–13 year olds (Morris *et al.* 1999), especially where the policy was adopted with enthusiasm by careers coordinators. A number of conditions must be met to leverage policy implementation using a top-down managerial approach, including a clear vision, action to change the culture of the school and appropriate resources, but even that may not be sufficient (Trowler 2003). The phenomenological or bottom-up perspective on policy implementation emphasises the importance of understanding the roles and values of the different groups of operational staff whose actions are critical to the success of the policy.

Implementation gap

In the transition from 'policy-making' to 'policy implementation', problems tend to arise. The time delay between the announcement of a new policy and its roll-out in schools is one such difficulty. In recent years, schools have been bombarded with policy initiatives and CLD has been known to lose out to competing priorities. An Ofsted survey in 1998, for example, found that 10 per cent of schools still had no careers library, even though funding for careers libraries had been available since 1994, and the provision of up-to-date careers information in schools had been made a statutory requirement in the 1997 Education Act.

Patchiness

Schools often have to respond selectively to new initiatives in order to reduce overload on staff. Deciding what the school will do, should do or could do becomes a political process. This mirrors the reality of policy-making at government level. It is often assumed that policy-making is incremental and coherent. In practice, it is often the result of negotiation, necessity and compromise.

Improvement

Policy initiatives alert schools to the need to do things differently and to the ways of doing things differently. The IAG strategy for schools (DCSF 2009b), for example, has tried to shift the emphasis away from reliance on the single guidance interview and matching approaches at decision and transition points. Starting earlier, using experiential approaches and engaging business and community partners are included in the strategy. Over the years, governments have used new policy initiatives to revive schools' flagging interest in CLD. In recent times, governments have appeared to 're-launch' CLD approximately every seven years (Working Together for a Better Future, DES 1987; Better Choices, DfEE 1994; careers education support programme 2001; Principles of Impartial Careers Education, DCSF 2009c)!

The impact of policy thinking on CLD

In the modern era, we can trace the influence of political ideals on CLD policy since the 1970s. The most consistent commentator on CLD policy has been Watts (e.g. 1995, 2008) with notable contributions by Bates (e.g. 1984), Harris (1999), Andrews (e.g. 2006) and others.

It was in the early 1970s that the idea of careers education developed as an optional part of the curriculum to furnish young people, especially school leavers, with the information and skills they needed to make informed choices. The decline of traditional industries, the raising of the school leaving age (RoSLA) and the expansion of pastoral care and support in comprehensive schools acted as a spur. Schools started to appoint careers teachers as opposed to relying on the informal assistance of interested teachers.

The acrimonious Schools Council Careers Education and Guidance Project (1971–77) exposed the lack of consensus about the scope and purpose of careers education (Harris 1999). This was also the time of the 'Great Debate' launched by the then prime minister James Callaghan (1976) which challenged schools to consider to what extent the curriculum prepared young people for the world of work and whether the knowledge and skills learnt were what employers needed. The careers field had its own great debate when Roberts challenged the primacy of career development theory by arguing that career guidance could do little to empower individual agency in the face of the constraints of the opportunity structure (Roberts 1982). When Law and Watts wrote *Schools, Careers and Community* (1977), a seminal work that has influenced the objectives of careers education to the present day, they were struck by the part that power relations played in the development of career guidance systems. In the mid-1980s, Bates (1984) referred to the chameleon-like character of careers education and guidance which seemed to change its complexion in the face of the prevailing demands of policy-makers. This malleability can be viewed both as a strength in the sense that careers education continues to demonstrate its relevance but also as a weakness in that it shows a lack of conviction about what it stands for, to the confusion of stakeholders.

The experience of the 1980s showed that the effectiveness of CEIAG policy can be affected by how it has been formulated. The Technical and Vocational Education Initiative (TVEI) from 1983 to 1993, for example, which promoted work-related learning in schools was managed quite successfully by the Manpower Services Commission (MSC) (Dale *et al.* 1990). The view at the time in the highest levels of government was that this policy could not be entrusted to the Department for Education and Science (DES) in case they dragged their feet. TVEI provided a strong impetus for careers work, as learners needed help in choosing subjects and courses wisely and in understanding the real-life relevance of what they were studying.

The DES at this time was moving in a different direction to the MSC. The ten subject National Curriculum that was announced in 1988 excluded careers education. Retrospectively, the National Curriculum Council delineated an infrastructure of cross-curricular themes, skills and dimensions that were supposed to permeate the subjects in the curriculum. Careers education and guidance became a cross-curricular theme (NCC 1990), but it remained a structurally weak element in the curriculum throughout the 1990s and received varying levels of attention from schools, largely because of the difficulty of establishing integrated careers work in the existing education climate. The career guidance integration project (Law and Evans 1984) had come up against this problem a few years earlier. However, a renewed focus on careers education was apparent in the series of curriculum guidance booklets produced by the government's main curriculum agency starting with *Looking Forward* (SCAA 1995).

Until 1995, the Department of Employment had responsibility for the careers service and the Department for Education had responsibility for careers education policy. This kept careers education and guidance (CEG) in a state of balanced tension between the world of work (the focus of the DoE) and the world of the learner and learning (the focus of the DfE). This did not in itself stop careers education becoming the poor relation of the curriculum, but when, in two stages, the departments were merged and the responsibility for careers education moved physically from the curriculum division of the DfEE office in London to the careers service division in Sheffield, it is arguable that, in the long term, careers education policy lost ground.

The most important effect of the New Right thinking of the 1990s was the decision to privatise the careers service by removing it from local authority control (Peck 2004). The influence of New Right educational ideas on CEIAG policy was also strongly reflected in two reports from the Confederation of British Industry (CBI) in the early 1990s. Routes for Success (1993) advanced the idea of 'Careership' as a formal period in which 16 to 19 year olds would be offered relevant qualifications and core skills, a Careership profile for planning and recording their learning, top quality and independent careers education and guidance, and financial credits to give them real influence and buying power in the education and training market. A Credit to Your Career (1994) advanced a number of proposals to stimulate a market in career guidance and give choice to young people and schools over which guidance providers to use.

The CBI's ideas required radical policy shifts and were never fully adopted, but the Conservative government of the day was strongly influenced by their thinking which was in keeping with the drive to promote the UK's global economic competitiveness. It was the conviction that CEG could contribute to the success of the competitiveness policy that persuaded the government to make careers education statutory for 14 to 16 year olds in 1997 (extended to 11 to 13 year olds in 2003).

The 1990s was an important stage in careers education becoming an emergent requirement for all learners. The most common way of providing careers education was through personal and social education (PSE), supplemented by work experience and other activities. When the government made citizenship statutory in 2004, careers education was squeezed since these activities often had to be provided without additional curriculum time. Meanwhile, the expansion of work-related learning (a statutory requirement at Key Stage 4 from 2004), enterprise education and financial capability was putting further pressure on an already overcrowded curriculum. The solution proposed in the 2007 revision of the National Curriculum was to integrate some of these elements and to create a non-statutory subject called personal, social, health and economic education (PSHEe) with two programmes of study. One programme was for personal well-being, which implicitly picked up the equality of opportunity and decision-making elements of CLD, and the other for economic well-being and financial capability which addressed the careers, work-related, enterprise and personal finance elements of PSHEe. The Labour government went further by proposing to make PSHEe statutory in 2009. In the 2007 National Curriculum, an attempt was made to tackle the problem of the structural weakness of cross-curricular elements such as careers education by encouraging schools to introduce thematic learning alongside subject-based learning approaches (see Chapter 5).

The external support for CLD in schools from the local service set up to provide career guidance also waned as a result of the demise of the careers service and the reduction in the universal provision of careers advice under Connexions (2000–01). In 2000, 'Connexions Partnerships' were created in England. These emerged as partnerships of a range of organisations and services for young people from age 13 to 19. They subsumed all publicly funded careers work and, with the overall aim of reducing those young people not in employment, education or training (NEET), addressed wider issues amongst disaffected youth such as housing, relationships and substance misuse. The targeting of those most likely to become NEET meant that mainstream services were squeezed.

The advent of Connexions shows that policy-making is not necessarily rational or incremental. The policy that the Labour government of 1997 was expected to implement was the Byers–Gee plan hatched in opposition, but it was dropped in favour of the Connexions policy that was conceived initially not in the DfEE but in the Cabinet Office.

In part, concerns about the impact of Connexions on CEG were muted by a growing acceptance that public services should be targeted at need and should not provide blanket provision that was often wasteful. ICT was embraced as a way of cutting costs in providing elements of the universal service. However, Watts (2001) argued that the essential design flaw of Connexions was that it was conceived as a targeted service rather than as a universal but differentiated service.

What Connexions did add to the policy ideals that impacted on CEG was a concern for social justice. The Labour governments from 1997 allied the previous policy of promoting economic competitiveness with a commitment to equality of opportunity and social inclusion. However, reconciling the demands of economic development and social justice has proved remarkably difficult (Irving 2005) and the problems of those who are not in education, employment or training (NEET) have been difficult to overcome, especially during the recession and subsequent period of tight budgetary constraint. In the meantime, evidence was emerging in the late noughties that, with more limited access to career guidance, more young people were less well-prepared as career decision-makers. First-year higher education drop-out rates in England, for example, rose to 22 per cent in 2008 according to the Commons Public Accounts Committee (February 2008).

On the education side, the publication of Every Child Matters in 2004 marked a new phase of converting traditional education departments into integrated children's services. The Every Child Matters framework built on the recommendations of Lord Laming's report following the death of Victoria Climbié in 2003. Although the focus of this investigation was understandably that of child protection, it had implications for all organisations providing services to children and young people, in that it revealed the woefully inadequate protocols for information sharing and recording. The resulting framework proposed five outcomes for children and young people against which the performance of services including schools could be measured. These outcomes have provided a useful focus for CLD; it being one of the few aspects of provision that could genuinely contribute to all five outcomes (see Box 3.1).

Box 3.1 CLD and well-being outcomes for children and young people

Well-being outcomes	Link to CLD
Be safe	Sound decision-making skills help young people to make choices that will keep them safe, whether those decisions are to do with their behaviour, relationships or activities in the workplace.
Be healthy	Similarly, the element of decision-making in CLD enables young people to make informed choices about diet, drugs, exercise and occupational health.
Enjoy and achieve	This outcome clearly has its focus on young people's learning and attainment in school, but it is also the key to career well-being. Good CLD provision motivates and inspires young people, builds their confidence and enables them to choose opportunities wisely.
Make a positive contribution	This refers to the way that people interact with each other in their organisations and communities. 'Career' is fundamentally about how individuals attend not only to their personal well-being but contribute to the well-being of others through the work they do.
Achieve economic well-being	Preparing to manage and sustain one's own economic livelihood is perhaps the most obvious link with CLD. It is composed of two parts: functioning well and being happy.

The 14–19 Education and Skills White Paper (DCSF 2005) signalled the government's intention to introduce far-reaching changes to the opportunities for this age group. The reforms involved modifications to GCSEs and A levels, the introduction of a new diploma in fourteen subjects at three levels, an expansion of apprenticeships and the creation of Foundation Learning for young people with learning difficulties and disabilities. Since no single institution could offer the full entitlement to young people, the reforms also required schools to collaborate in consortium-type arrangements. These reforms created a need for greatly improved careers education, information, advice and guidance (CEIAG) to help learners, and their parents/carers, to understand and benefit from the changes. One of the government's concerns was that young people might not receive impartial careers education or get to hear about opportunities that are relevant to them such as apprenticeships. With this in mind, they passed legislation in 2009 to require schools to provide impartial careers education and to give information about apprenticeships. They backed this up with the publication of a new IAG strategy (DCSF 2009b) and statutory guidance on impartial careers education (DCSF 2009c).

Policy orientations of CEIAG

By understanding the policy orientations of CEIAG, schools will be able to recognise the characteristics of their own CLD policy. They will be able to debate whether to change the emphasis of what they are doing and how to respond appropriately to national policy initiatives.

Watts and Sultana (2004) identified three main categories of policy goals of national career guidance services that can also be applied at the school level. The first category relates to helping learners negotiate and navigate their way through the education system as efficiently as possible. The second relates to helping young people prepare to enter the labour market and to become economically productive citizens. CLD oils the wheels of the labour market and helps to reduce inefficient job-seeking behaviour. The third is about supporting socially disadvantaged individuals and groups in getting access to opportunities. Countries prioritise these different sets of goals at different times and find it a challenge to maintain a balance between them. This is an issue for schools as well.

Watts (1996; adapted from Watts and Herr 1976) has also suggested four proto-typical socio-political orientations of CLD (see Figure 3.1) which will influence the exact nature of the policy goals that a career guidance service or school will choose to pursue.

One dimension of the matrix looks at whether the intention of CLD is to maintain the status quo or to precipitate change. The other dimension asks whether the core focus is on the individual or on society. The liberal or non-directive approach is supportive of individuals in a laissez-faire way – it is up to them whether they 'sink or swim'. The conservative approach serves the current needs of society by helping people to fit in where they can be economically useful. A progressive approach deliberately sets out to make a difference to individual lives by raising aspirations and supporting ambition. A radical approach sets its sights on making a difference to the lives of individuals within groups in society.

Schools can use this matrix to analyse the balance of elements in their CLD provision and to assess their scope for change, but it is very important to check whether the rhetoric of the CLD policy is matched by the reality.

Influencing policy and policy-makers

CLD professionals often feel that CEIAG does not receive sufficient policy attention. We have seen earlier that the focus on CEIAG waxes and wanes. Although complaints about policy neglect are probably mirrored across all areas of the curriculum, what are some of the reasons why CLD sometimes feels marginalised?

	Core focus on society	Core focus on individual
Change	Radical (Social Change)	Progressive (Individual Change)
Status Quo	Conservative (Social Control)	Liberal (Non-Directive)

Figure 3.1 Socio-political orientations of CLD (after Watts and Herr 1976)

- Careers are ubiquitous so it is easy to take CLD for granted.
- Career is a nebulous and complex concept and so the scope and value of CLD is not well understood by other staff.
- It lacks the status of an exam subject.
- Schools do not accept full responsibility for CLD as they deliver it in partnership with career guidance services.
- Resource inputs (staffing, curriculum time, etc.) are inadequate.

The onus is on careers professionals to make the case for policy attention for CLD. This is difficult given the relatively weak professionalisation of careers specialists in schools. Many miss out on the stage of professional identity formation in initial training because there is no route in initial training for them. On the job, they are often isolated unless they join a professional association or go to network meetings of careers practitioners where they can learn more about what careers professionals do and lobby to influence policy at the local level or to contribute local responses to national policy consultations on CEIAG. (A list of key organisations is provided at the end of this chapter.) When their horizons are bounded by the schools they work for, they may have very little commitment to the wider professional field or awareness of what is happening at both a national or a European policy level.[1] Engaging with policy debate and providing a counterpoint to it through a strong professional identity is vital as there can be few questions more important than who gets to do what in our society.

Discussion points

1   How effective is your school policy for CLD (assuming you have one)?
2   Who or what are the influences on the CLD provision in your school?

Note

1   The European Union has published resolutions in 2004 and 2008. The new resolution encourages the lifelong acquisition of career management skills, access by all citizens to guidance services, the development of quality assurance of guidance provision and coordination and cooperation among the various national, regional and local stakeholders.

References

Andrews, D. (2006) 'A short history of careers education policy in England', *Career Research and Development*, 15: 5–8.

Bates, I. (1984) 'From vocational guidance to life skills: Historical perspectives on careers education', in I. Bates, J. Clarke, P. Cohen, D. Finn, R. Moore and P. Wills, *Schooling for the Dole? The New Vocationalis*, London: Macmillan.

Becta (2001) *Connecting Careers & ICT*, Sheffield: Connexions Service National Unit.

Dale, R. *et al.* (1990) *The TVEI Story: Policy, Practice and Preparation for the Workforce*, Milton Keynes: Open University Press.

DCSF (2005) *14–19 Education and Skills*, London: DCSF. Online: www.dcsf.gov.uk/14-19/documents/14-19whitepaper.pdf (accessed 14 February 2010).

DCSF (2009a) *A Guide to the Law for School Governors*, London: DCSF. Online: www.governornet.co.uk/linkAttachments/GTTL%2024.10.09.pdf (accessed 14 February 2010).

DCSF (2009b) *Quality, Choice and Aspiration. A Strategy for Young People's Information, Advice and Guidance.* Online: www.publications.dcsf.gov.uk/eOrderingDownload/IAG-Report-V2.pdf (accessed 12 February 2010).

DCSF (2009c) *Statutory Guidance: Impartial Careers Education,* Nottingham: DCSF. Online: http://publications.teachernet.gov.uk/eOrderingDownload/00978-2009DOM-EN.pdf(accessed 3 February 2010).

DES/DoE/Welsh Office (1987) *Working Together for a Better Future.* London: Central Office of Information.

DfEE (1994) *Better Choices: The Principles,* London: DfEE.

Harris, S. (1999) *Careers Education: Contesting Policy and Practice,* London: Paul Chapman Publishing.

Irving, B. (2005) 'Social justice: a context for career education and guidance', in B.A. Irving and B. Malik (eds.) *Critical Reflections on Career Education and Guidance: Promoting Social Justice within a Global Economy,* London: RoutledgeFalmer.

Kidd, J. (2006) 'Exploring career well-being in two cultures', *Career Research and Development: The NICEC Journal,* 16: 5–9.

Kidd, J.M., Killeen, J., Jarvis, J. and Offer, M. (1994) 'Is guidance an applied science? The role of theory in the careers guidance interview', *British Journal of Guidance and Counselling,* 22(3): 385–403.

Law, B. and Evans, K. (1984) *Career Guidance Integration Project,* Hatfield: NICEC.

Law, B. and Watts, A.G. (1977) *Schools, Careers and Community,* London: CIO Publishing.

Morris, M., Lines, A. and Golden, S. (1999) *The Impact of Careers Education and Guidance on Young People in Years 9 and 10: a Follow Up Study (RD 20),* Sheffield: DfEE.

NCC (1990) *Curriculum Guidance 6: Careers Education and Guidance,* York: National Curriculum Council.

Ofsted (1998) *Careers Education and Guidance in Secondary Schools,* London: HMSO.

Peck, D. (2004) *Careers Services: History, Policy and Practice in the United Kingdom,* London: RoutledgeFalmer.

Roberts, K. (1982) 'The sociology of work entry and occupational choice', in A.G. Watts, D.E. Super and J.M. Kidd (eds.) *Career Development in Britain: Some Contributions to Theory and Practice,* Cambridge: CRAC.

SCAA (1995) *Looking Forward: Careers Education and Guidance in the Curriculum,* London: SCAA.

Trowler, P. (2003) *Education Policy,* 2nd edn, London: Routledge.

Watts, A.G. (1995) 'The Policy Context', in A. Barnes and D. Andrews (eds) *Developing Careers Education and Guidance in the Curriculum,* London: David Fulton.

Watts, A.G. (1996) 'Career guidance and public policy', in A.G. Watts, B. Law, J. Killeen, J.M. Kidd and R. Hawthorn, *Rethinking Careers Education and Guidance: Theory, Policy and Practice,* London: Routledge.

Watts, A.G. (2001) 'Career guidance and social exclusion: a cautionary tale', *British Journal of Guidance and Counselling,* 29(2): 157–176.

Watts, A.G. and Sultana, R.G. (2004) 'Career guidance policies in 37 countries: contrasts and common themes', *International Journal for Educational and Vocational Guidance,* 4(2–3): 105–122.

Watts, A.G. (2008) 'The partnership model for careers education and guidance: rise, decline – and fall?', *Career Research and Development,* 20: 4–8.

Professional organisations

Association of Career Professionals – www.acpinternational.org
Association for Careers Education and Guidance – www.aceg.org.uk
Institute of Career Guidance – www.icg-uk.org
Inspiring Futures (previously ISCO) – www.isco.org.uk

Part B

Practice

Chapter 4

Leadership and strategy

Promoting the career learning and development of young people through the formal education system presents formidable leadership and strategic management challenges. We examine some of the key elements of leadership and strategy as they apply to CLD and relate this to the performance of key tasks. The chapter concludes with a discussion of the main roles and responsibilities of a wide range of guidance and education professionals working as senior leaders, middle leaders and operational staff, not all of whom would readily class themselves as careers specialists.

Leadership and its importance

Effective leadership at all levels is widely recognised as the hallmark of a successful school. What leadership is and what makes a good leader are both hotly debated. West-Burnham (cited in Davies and Ellison 1997) attempted to show that leadership and management were distinctive but complementary activities (see Box 4.1).

Box 4.1 Management and leadership

Management is about:

- implementation
- operational issues
- transaction
- means
- systems
- doing things right

Leadership is about:

- vision
- strategic issues
- transformation
- ends
- people
- doing the right things

(West-Burnham in Davies and Ellison 1997)

Current thinking on leadership emphasises that it is not just a 'top-down' phenomenon. Senior leaders may have primary responsibility for strategy but middle leaders (e.g. careers coordinators) usually have a major input into strategy and are in any case largely responsible for its implementation. Educational leadership is distributed throughout a school and it is up to individuals to make effective use of the leadership authority they can legitimately claim.

Current thinking also emphasises that leaders should try to flex their leadership style to respond in a way that suits the needs of the situation and the people involved. How everyone else performs their leadership functions affects everyone else's leadership capacity and style. Joseph Nye, Distinguished Service Professor at Harvard University, writing about effective world leaders, defines this ability as 'contextual intelligence' – the intuitive diagnostic skill that helps you align your tactics with your objectives so that you get 'smart' strategies in different situations. Tannenbaum and Schmidt (1973) describe a continuum of leadership styles and it is helpful for leaders of CLD to reflect on the pros and cons of adopting these different styles to cope with the situations they face (see Box 4.2).

Box 4.2 Leadership styles

Style	*Definition*
Telling	Leader gives instructions and has a strong control instinct
Selling	Leader has clear views and values and attempts to convince others to follow
Consulting	Leader presents ideas, invites comments and suggestions, and reaches decisions by consensus
Sharing	Leader develops other staff and delegates actions and decisions within defined limits

(Tannenbaum and Schmidt 1973, cited in Field *et al.* 2000)

It is also widely acknowledged that leadership is a group dynamic in which followers formally or informally give their consent to be led. Harnessing this dynamic is one of the skills of leadership. Collarbone and Billingham (1998) draw a distinction between 'transactional' and 'transformational' leadership which provides further insights into how this consent might work (see Box 4.3). 'Transactional leadership' (based on the exchange relationships

---

Box 4.3 'Transformational' and 'transactional' leadership

Transformational leadership	Transactional leadership
• builds on the need for meaning	• builds on the need to get the job done and make a living
• preoccupied with purposes, values, morals and ethics	• preoccupied with power and position, politics and perks
• transcends daily affairs	• swamped in daily affairs
• orientated towards long term goals without compromising human values and principles	• orientated to short-term goals and hard data
• separates causes and symptoms and works at prevention	• confuses causes and symptoms and is concerned with treatment
• focuses more on missions and strategies for achieving them	• focuses on tactical issues
• makes full use of available human resources	• relies on human relations to oil human interactions
• designs and redesigns jobs to make them meaningful and challenging; realises human potential	• follows and fulfils role expectations by striving to work effectively within current systems
• aligns internal structures and systems to reinforce overarching values and goals	• supports structures and systems that reinforce the bottom line, maximise efficiency and guarantee short-term gains

(Collarbone and Billingham 1998)

---

between the leader and the follower) can be contrasted with 'transformational leadership' (based on the ability of an individual to envision a new social condition and communicate this vision to followers).

School improvement researchers emphasise the value of 'transformational leadership'. 'Transformational' leaders have the ability to inspire a shared vision, to empower staff and to 'raise everyone's game'. It is the way in which these leaders transform the feelings, attitudes and beliefs of students, colleagues and partners that is particularly relevant to improvement in CLD.

Careers leaders will sometimes need to reflect on the basis of their power or authority to make things happen. Power can be represented on a spectrum from 'clout' to 'wisdom' (see Box 4.4).

Box 4.4 Spectrum of power

Reward power   is based on the belief of followers that the leader has access to valued rewards which will be dispensed in return for compliance with instructions

Coercive power   is based on the belief of followers that the leader can administer penalties or sanctions that are considered to be unwelcome

Referent power   is based on the belief of followers that the leader has desirable abilities and personality traits that can and should be copied

Legitimate power   is based on the belief of followers that the leader has a position of authority in the organisational hierarchy which gives them the right to issue orders with which followers have an obligation to comply

Expert power   is based on the belief of followers that the leader has superior knowledge relevant to the task in hand

(French and Raven 1959)

Careers coordinators usually have limited access to the 'harder' forms of power but they have more scope to use the 'softer' forms of power to win support for what they want to achieve. Softer forms of power focus on motivation and work best when the interests of the leader coincide with the needs and interests of those they are seeking to influence. This is relevant to strategic leadership as CEIAG is traditionally a 'goodwill curriculum' (Harris 1999) which relies on the coordinator negotiating support from colleagues within the school.

Strategic management of CLD

Strategy is about knowing what to achieve, being able to justify the direction and finding the best way to get there.

The need for a well-developed strategy relates to the complexity of CLD. Careers work is relevant to the needs of all young people in a school, it is delivered across the curriculum by a wide range of staff and it requires the contribution of a wide range of internal and external partners. Moreover, it must respond to national and local policy initiatives while staying focused on the needs of young people, the school and its community.

A useful model for strategic planning of CLD at the school level is the seven 'S's framework developed by McKinsey & Company (1982). It shows the relationship of strategy to six other elements or variables that need to be aligned to improve school performance (see Fig. 4.1).

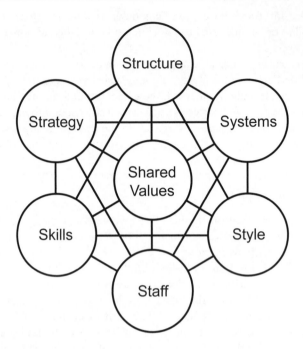

Figure 4.1 The seven 'S's framework

The benefits of using the seven 'S's tool for school leaders are:

- It focuses on the seven key elements that determine whether CLD provision is effective or not – that is, it can be used to diagnose problems and develop a strategy for improvement.
- It emphasises that the successful implementation of CLD activities requires all these elements to be coordinated and aligned.
- It acts as a reminder of the complexity of change – that is, to improve CLD provision may involve working on aspects of all these elements.

Box 4.5 provides a checklist of CLD issues to consider under each of the elements in the framework. It can be used to gather evidence of the effectiveness of current strategy.

Box 4.5 Seven 'S's framework checklist

Strategy

Check:

- Is the CLD policy up to date?
- Is the CLD development plan in operation and linked to the overall school improvement plan?
- Is CLD integrated into the school's curriculum and learning design; for example, providing coherence across personal development (PD) and work-related learning and enterprise education (WRLE)?

- Are collaborative partnerships actively managed; for example, home–school, business and community?
- Are resources sufficient and deployed efficiently; for example, staffing, curriculum time, accommodation, equipment?

Structure

Check:

- Is the staffing organisation for CLD 'fit for purpose'?
- Are roles and responsibilities for CLD clear?
- Are reporting and decision-making lines clear?

Systems

Check:

- Are arrangements in place for performance management and review of leaders responsible for CLD?
- Are staff guidelines in place; for example, for knowing how and when to refer students for specialist help, writing references, visiting students on work experience?
- Is the CLD service model explicit and well understood by students, parents/carers and staff?
- Are teaching and learning methods and techniques fit for purpose; for example, supporting the personalisation of learning?
- Have the learner voice and parent voice been activated?
- Is CLD regularly monitored, reviewed and evaluated?
- Does record-keeping support assessment for learning and effectiveness and improvement?
- Are day-to-day administrative processes and procedures sound?
- Are procedures and systems in place for variations; for example, short-stay pupils, looked after young people and learners with special educational needs?

Style

Check:

- How effective is leadership at all levels?
- Are communications open and frequent?
- Is the school open and responsive to change in its CLD provision?
- Are young people actively involved in the design, delivery and evaluation of the CLD provision?
- Is school self-review and evaluation of CLD viewed positively?
- Are safeguarding and other checks in place; for example, impartiality, confidentiality?

Staff

Check:

- Does induction for new staff include an explanation of how young people's CLD needs are met?

> • Do all relevant staff have access to continuing professional development and support?
>
> **Shared values**
>
> Check:
>
> • Is a commitment to CLD part of the shared understanding of all staff?
>
> **Skills**
>
> Check:
>
> • Is the skills set of the careers team up to date and does it cover all the functional areas of careers work in the school?
> • Do subject teachers and tutors have the appropriate level of skills?

Key strategic management tasks

Developing a vision

A report by the National College (2009) identified purposeful leadership and visioning as the most important factors in effective leadership of information, advice and guidance. A vision is a general statement that describes where the school is going. Its purpose is to clarify the overall direction and mission of the school and to inspire and challenge those it is intended to motivate. Having a vision provides a valuable compass for those managing and implementing the CLD programme; and creates confidence in young people and parents and carers. Vision statements are strongly influenced by values and beliefs which in relation to CLD will include references to issues such as:

• unlocking potential – for example, to help young people become everything that they can be;
• promoting autonomy – for example, to enable young people to determine and manage their own careers;
• finding happiness – for example, to create the conditions for young people to achieve personal and economic well-being;
• making progress – for example, to help young people take the next steps in learning and work;
• achieving wider social, economic and environmental purposes – for example, to promote fairness, inclusion and diversity; to help young people become enterprising and employable; to encourage young people to choose green and sustainable careers; and to encourage young people to contribute to the well-being of others.

The role of the leader for CLD includes conducting the debate on the direction of careers work in the school, aligning it with the school's overall vision and mission and communicating the vision to all stakeholders.

Formulating policy

Policy is one of the key elements of strategy related to vision. Most schools and colleges already have a policy for career-related learning but is it really necessary? Hewton (1988) suggests that the advantages of preparing and agreeing a policy are that it is:

- a focusing device on curriculum areas, procedures, etc.;
- a way of ordering needs – that is, a form of organisational analysis;
- a means of sharing ideas, airing views, debating differences, settling differences, reaching consensus and building collegiality;
- a direction finder – that is, requiring a statement of aims;
- a co-ordinating mechanism for linking disparate activities;
- a form of commitment;
- an instrument of communication.

CLD as a contested area of school life benefits from having a policy statement because the formal adoption of policy is a way of signing up all stakeholders and players to its implementation. If CLD is part of a wider policy framework for economic well-being, PSHEe or personal development, it is essential that the CLD element that is to be integrated into this wider frame has been properly differentiated in the planning of the policy so that CLD does not end up being 'everywhere and nowhere' in the curriculum!

When developing policy for CLD, it is also vital for schools to consider their wider 'mission' when framing their goals for CLD. Faith schools and specialist schools, for example, will want to reflect their particular standpoint or specialism in their CLD policy. The link between the policy for CLD and other relevant policies such as teaching and learning, assessment and equality needs to be made explicit. In order that the policy for CLD supports the priorities in the school improvement plan, it is also desirable that the policy for CLD is revised and approved by the headteacher and governors at least every two years.

For policy to be successful, it is important to have an effective policy-making process which involves key stakeholders. While the school may have its own 'house style' for the way that policy statements are presented, a policy is likely to have sections which cover:

- the policy vision;
- purpose and aims of the policy (including a commitment to meeting statutory responsibilities);
- identification of the general and particular needs of individuals and groups in the school;
- the commitment and deployment of resources (including staffing and curriculum time);
- partnerships (including the engagement of young people, parents/carers and employers);
- the relationship to other policies;
- the arrangements for monitoring, reviewing and evaluating provision.

Development planning

Surveys repeatedly show a wide variation in the delivery and quality of careers education from comprehensive, planned programmes cross-referenced to appropriate standards to more informal arrangements (e.g. Ofsted 2010). Effective development planning ensures a more focused approach to improving CLD while maintaining the effectiveness of current provision.

A suggested structure for an annual development plan is a table with the following headings:

- Goals (a manageable but challenging number of priorities for the development of CLD linked to the school improvement plan, where appropriate)
- Actions (the steps needed to achieve each goal)
- By when? (the deadlines for achieving each goal)
- Led by? (the individual or team that will take the lead on working towards the achievement of each goal – there to encourage leaders to delegate responsibility, where possible)
- Resources (money, time and staffing needed to achieve each goal)
- Success criteria (indicators that will enable the school to know when the development has been achieved)
- Evaluation (for reviewing the outcomes of the planned development).

Deploying staff and resources

The effective deployment of staff and resources is a strategic management task. Every staffing model has its 'pros' and 'cons' and the challenge for leaders is how to maximise the advantages and minimise the disadvantages of the approach they adopt. Appointing a specialist CLD team, for example, helps staff to gain experience and build their expertise, but this is less likely to happen if individuals with slack on their timetable are 'press-ganged' into the team and if it discourages other staff from making appropriate contributions. Tutor and mentor-based models link pastoral care and support with CLD activities, but tutors and mentors may feel that they have insufficient time and expertise to provide careers education. Often, schools adopt hybrid staffing models that are a pragmatic response to the issue and reveal much about the culture and stage of development of the school.

Similarly, an effective approach to resource management requires more than a reactive approach to budgeting and financial planning. It is also about, for example, making effective use of time, succession planning and proactively investing in new technology to harness e-learning and e-guidance approaches.

Monitoring, reviewing and evaluating provision

The task of monitoring, reviewing and evaluating CLD provision is discussed in detail in Chapter 9.

Managing change

Continuing change in CLD provision often appears to be the norm and CLD leaders need to manage the processes of change in order to successfully bring about improvements. Michael Fullan has written extensively about educational change. In one of his earlier works from 1987 he identified three groups of factors that are involved in bringing about successful change (see Box 4.6).

Non-strategic change often breaks down when the careers coordinator or other promoter of the change leaves their post. Fullan (1989) emphasises the importance of embedding change so that it becomes something that the school stands for. Getting senior leadership support for the planned change, raising the awareness and interest of those who will be affected by the change, providing information, preparing them for implementing the change and supporting them during the early phases of implementation will all pay dividends. By then, the change will have become part of their routine practice!

Box 4.6 Factors in bringing about successful change

Initiation factors

There are four requirements:

1 Educational need should be linked to an agenda of political (high-profile) need.
2 A clear model should exist for the proposed change.
3 There needs to be a strong advocate for the change.
4 There should be an early active initiation establishing initial commitment, as an elaborate planning stage is wasteful of energy.

Implementation factors

Some critical needs include:

1 Careful orchestration: implementation requires the clear direction of many players; a group is needed to oversee the implementation plan and carry it through.
2 The correct alchemy of pressure and support.
3 Early rewards for implementers.
4 Ongoing in-service education and training (INSET), to maintain commitment as behaviours often change before beliefs.

Institutionalisation factors

An innovation will be more successful if:
1 It becomes embedded into the fabric of everyday practice.
2 It is clearly linked to classroom practice.
3 It is in widespread use across several classrooms and schools.
4 It is not contending with conflicting priorities.
5 It is subject to continuing INSET for new staff, to consolidate commitment.

Key people

The strategic leadership of CLD in most schools is shared between a number of key players, including the following.

Governors

Complying with the statutory requirements for careers education and having regard to the statutory guidance (DCSF 2009c) is the duty of the governing body and head teacher of every school. The governors' briefing in the resource pack which accompanies the statutory guidance suggests that governors should:

• consider the information and advice in the statutory guidance and resources pack;
• clarify arrangements for the delivery of careers education and personalised information, advice and guidance (CEIAG) within the school and plan for provision to be reviewed in the light of the statutory guidance;

- ensure that the review of provision will be rigorous and agree arrangements for its findings to be discussed with the governing body;
- consider appointing a governor with special responsibility for careers education;
- ask the headteacher to include feedback to governors on CEIAG in their termly reports;
- ensure that the governing body discusses CEIAG and pupil destinations at least once a year.

Headteachers and senior leaders

The *Statutory Guidance: Impartial Careers Education* (DCSF 2009c) identifies welve key points for headteachers to consider, many of them designed to encourage headteachers to manage careers education in a more strategic way. The statutory guidance recommends that the headteacher should identify a senior member of staff to lead and be accountable for the development of careers education and a work-related learning development plan linked to the school improvement plan. Every initiative from central government seems to carry the proviso that it needs to be coordinated by a senior leader which understandably presents schools with a considerable challenge, but the argument here is a strong one. CLD needs to be at the centre of the agenda for a number of reasons, including the raising of the participation age to 18 by 2015, the skills agenda, the 11–19 reforms and the changing world of work. The government recommendation is also linked to concerns about the effectiveness of careers coordination.

Middle leaders

The Statutory Guidance (DCSF 2009c) suggests that 'senior leaders with overall responsibility for ensuring high-quality careers education and IAG may choose to devolve some of their responsibilities to a middle leader (the 'careers leader' or 'careers coordinator')' (p. 35). It draws on recent research including a DCSF-commissioned survey of careers coordinators (DCSF 2009a), which highlights the safeguards that need to be put in place to ensure that middle leaders can perform effectively, namely:

- active and committed leadership of CEIAG by the headteacher and senior leader with designated overall responsibility;
- access to training and development to ensure that they have the skills and knowledge they need to perform effectively and to provide support for others involved in providing carers education;
- time for the careers coordinator to undertake their duties effectively;
- advice and support from the local Connexions service.

Careers Coordinators in Schools (DCSF 2009a) revealed the need for action on the qualification, skills and the role of careers coordinators. The report showed the diversification in the recruitment of careers coordinators and in the construction of roles in CEIAG in the preceding five years. In the past, the careers coordinator was nearly always a qualified teacher but this study showed that just over one quarter (26 per cent) were from business and industry, learning support, careers advising and other professional backgrounds. While coordinators from non-teaching backgrounds bring other valuable skills to the role, they may find it difficult to fulfil the curriculum leadership aspects of the role without access to suitable training and development opportunities.

The report also showed that, on average, respondents held four roles in addition to that of careers coordinator. Collectively, they mentioned over forty different roles. This illustrates the variety of solutions that schools have adopted in terms of leading and managing CLD. On the whole, respondents felt that their additional roles were complementary to their roles as careers coordinators but over half (54 per cent) said that they did not have enough time to manage CEIAG in their school.

Less than one-third of careers coordinators reported that they had a qualification (30 per cent) compared to 45 per cent in 2001. The creation of a route in initial teacher training is long overdue but most practitioners manage to learn on the job. Whether this is sufficient to meet the increasing demands of the role is questionable. In the report, 16 per cent said that they did not feel up to date with changes in CEIAG. Coordinators also reported barriers to taking a qualification – 53 per cent cited lack of time but 20 per cent said their school would not be able to release them to study and a further 20 per cent did not know there were any qualifications available. Being new to the role (25 per cent) and perceiving the absence of a clear career path for careers coordinators (20 per cent) were further disincentives.

Training and skills deficits, role overload and lack of time are not the only barriers to careers coordinators providing strategic leadership. The report highlighted other issues including:

- the need to raise the status of careers education and careers coordinators;
- careers coordinators who were responsible for Years 7 to 11 but not for post-16 students;
- the majority of careers coordinators undertook strategic management tasks such as preparing CEIAG development plans, advising senior leaders on CEIAG policy, priorities and resources; and monitoring, reviewing and evaluating provision. However, not all of them felt confident in carrying out such tasks and a significant minority did not perform them.

Schein's (1990) theory of career anchors can help us understand why some careers coordinators engage in strategic leadership tasks that are of little interest to them. Individuals whose principal career interests and values are related to technical and functional competence (i.e. being a CLD specialist) rather than to the exercise of managerial competence will nevertheless be prepared to perform strategic leadership tasks as a means to an end if it will help them to achieve goals in their own area of technical expertise.

A further illustration of why coordinators need to engage in leadership and strategy comes from what we know about 'organisational knowledge'. Field *et al.* (2000) make the point that organisations know some things but not others. What a school knows about CLD, for example, is the result of a long process of change management in which thinking about the scope and value of CLD has become embedded in the culture of the school. Astute coordinators will realise that they are one of the gatekeepers of this process and, therefore, they need to be proactive in their role as champions of CLD for young people. To help them make the case for involving all staff, one of the professional duties in *Teachers' Pay and Conditions* (DCSF 2009b) that teachers in England and Wales may be required to perform is:

> providing guidance and advice to pupils on educational and social matters and on their further education and future careers, including information about sources of more expert advice on specific questions; making relevant records and reports.
>
> (para. 72.2.2)

Successive professional development frameworks have attempted to map what staff leading and managing CLD in schools need to learn (see Box 4.7).

Box 4.7 Professional development frameworks for staff leading and managing CLD in schools

1 DfEE (1997) *Better Choices: Key areas for professional development for careers co-ordinators in schools.*

2 NACGT/TTA (1999, revised 2001) *National Standards for Subject Leaders: exemplified for the role of careers co-ordinator.*

3 The 2006 revised national occupational standards for Advice and Guidance from ENTO (The Employment National Training Organisation) (www.ento.co.uk/standards/index.php?catalogue=ag).

4 The *National Framework for Professional Qualifications in Careers Education and Guidance in England* (2008, 2nd edn) (www.cegnet.co.uk/files/CEGNET0001/resources/586.doc).

Box 4.8 A draft framework of learning outcomes for lead careers specialists in schools (NFER/NICEC, 2010)

Core outcomes

1 Understand the career learning and development needs of young people in the school.
2 Know the explanations in careers theory and research that support effective practice.
3 Know how to lead and manage CEIAG in the school.
4 Develop and maintain effective systems and procedures to support the delivery of CEIAG.
5 Know how to use ICT to provide effective CEIAG activities.
6 Communicate the benefits of participating in the CEIAG provision to young people and their supporters.
7 Collaborate with professional colleagues and partners in and beyond the school to enhance CEIAG provision.
8 Ensure high standards of professional behaviour and practice.
9 Challenge stereotypes, raise aspirations and promote fairness, inclusion and respect for diversity.
10 Continue to develop professionally as a careers leader.

Main outcomes

11 Assist the school in developing and implementing its CEIAG vision and strategy.
12 Monitor, review, evaluate and quality assure CEIAG provision to support continuing effectiveness and improvement.
13 Engage professional, home, community and business partners in CEIAG.
14 Design, plan and develop the programme of CEIAG activities.
15 Know, select and use teaching, learning and assessment methods for CEIAG that are fit for purpose.
16 Select, develop and present careers information resources.
17 Provide and facilitate careers information, advice and guidance.
18 Enable the professional development of staff involved in CEIAG.

An updated but as yet unpublished draft framework of learning outcomes for careers leaders is summarised in Box 4.8. It was developed as part of the careers coordinators in schools project (DCSF 2009a). One of its uses is to audit who does what to ensure that all the functional areas in the leadership and management are covered by post-holders. This framework maps all the functional areas associated with the leadership and management of CLD and recognises that schools have flexibility over the way these functions are shared between different roles in the school.

Conclusion

The changes taking place in careers coordination in schools have brought challenges as well as benefits to schools, but too many issues remain unresolved. Schools know very little themselves about the efficacy of the different models of coordination and leadership that they are adopting. Access to suitable qualifications is problematic in some areas and the motivation of coordinators is mixed. These are among the issues that the national taskforce on the careers profession (2010) was set up to address.

Discussion points

1   Imagine you have been appointed to work in a new school that to start with only has 11–13 year olds (Y7–9 in England) but will eventually become an 11–19 school. Devise a strategic plan for embedding CEIAG in the curriculum of the developing school.

2   Recall an occasion when you were called upon to act as a consultant on CEIAG to a subject department or a tutor team. What skills did you use and what worked well?

References

Collarbone, P. and Billingham, M. (1998) *Leadership and Our Schools*, School Improvement Network Research Matters No. 8, London: University of London Institute of Education.

Davies, B. and Ellison, L. (1997) *School Leadership for the 21st Century*, London: Routledge.

DCSF (2009a) *Careers Coordinators in Schools*, London: DCSF. Online: http://publications.dcsf.gov.uk/eOrderingDownload/DCSF-RR171.pdf (accessed 14 February 2010).

DCSF (2009b) *School Teachers' Pay and Conditions Document 2009 and Guidance on School Teachers' Pay and Conditions*, Norwich: TSO. Online: www.teachernet.gov.uk/_doc/14150/STPCD%202009.pdf (accessed 14 February 2010).

DCSF (2009c) *Statutory Guidance: Impartial Careers Education*, Nottingham: DCSF. Online: http://publications.teachernet.gov.uk/eOrderingDownload/00978-2009DOM-EN.pdf (accessed 3 February 2010).

Field, K., Holden, P. and Lawlor, H. (2000) *Effective Subject Leadership*, London: Routledge.

French, J. and Raven, B. (1959) 'The bases of social power', in D. Cartwright (ed.) *Studies in Social Power*, Ann Arbor, MI: Institute for Social Research.

Fullan, M. (1989) 'Managing Curriculum Change' in M. Preedy (ed.) *Approaches to Curriculum Management*, Milton Keynes: Open University.

Harris, S. (1999) *Careers Education: Contesting Policy and Practice*, London: Paul Chapman Publishing.

Hewton, E. (1988) *School-focused Staff Development*, Brighton: Falmer Press.

National College (2009) *Impartial Careers Education: Effective Leadership of Information, Advice and Guidance,* Nottingham: National College.

NFER/NICEC (2010) *Qualifications for Careers Leaders – A framework of learning outcomes for lead careers specialists in schools.* Online: not yet available

Ofsted (2010) *Moving through the System: Preparation for Economic Well-being and for Life and Work.* Online: www.ofsted.gov.uk/content/download/10961/130113/file/Moving%20through%20the%20system%20–%20information,%20advice%20and%20guidance.pdf.

Schein, E. (1990) *Career Anchors (Discovering your Real Values),* San Francisco: Jossey-Bass Pfeiffer.

Chapter 5

Career learning and development in the curriculum

Schools have an important role in meeting young people's career learning and development (CLD) needs through the curriculum. This chapter discusses different curriculum structures where career learning can be facilitated, and outlines an effective model of curriculum planning for developing a school's careers education provision. It argues that a narrow instrumental approach to CLD is not sufficient to prepare young people for twenty-first-century lives and that more powerful cognitive and affective approaches are needed. The chapter concludes by raising key issues for curriculum leaders seeking to improve CLD in their schools.

Statutory requirements and guidance

Although policy and practice vary considerably, the importance of making curricular provision for careers education is recognised in the education systems of most developed countries. In England, for example, careers education is statutory for 11 to 16 year olds in England in maintained schools (OPSI 1997, 2003), and the DCSF had an ambition to extend the duty to 18 by 2015 in line with the raising of the participation age (DCSF 2009). The role of careers education has been extended to ensure that schools provide impartial information on all aspects of education and training, including apprenticeships (OPSI 2008, 2009). Its role has also been strengthened in relation to raising aspirations, challenging stereotypes and broadening horizons. The Labour government's plans to start even earlier by making personal, social, health and economic education statutory at Key Stages 1–4 had to be dropped in April 2010 in the absence of Opposition support for the measure.

Understanding careers education in the curriculum

The curriculum is often defined as the sum total of the teaching and learning experiences planned for learners, but this can be misleading. Curriculum planners know the difference between the 'received' and the 'intended' curriculum, and that the relationship between them needs to be managed carefully. Similarly, important learning is transmitted through informal and 'hidden' curriculum processes over which schools may exert some influence but not overall control.

These issues are relevant to the way that curriculum leaders for careers need to understand and manage the 'CLD curriculum'. Figure 5.1 shows the main curriculum structures through which CLD is provided.

The CLD curriculum is an amalgam of five interlinked parts that can be compared to the sections of an orchestra: the challenge for the curriculum leader for careers is how to orches-

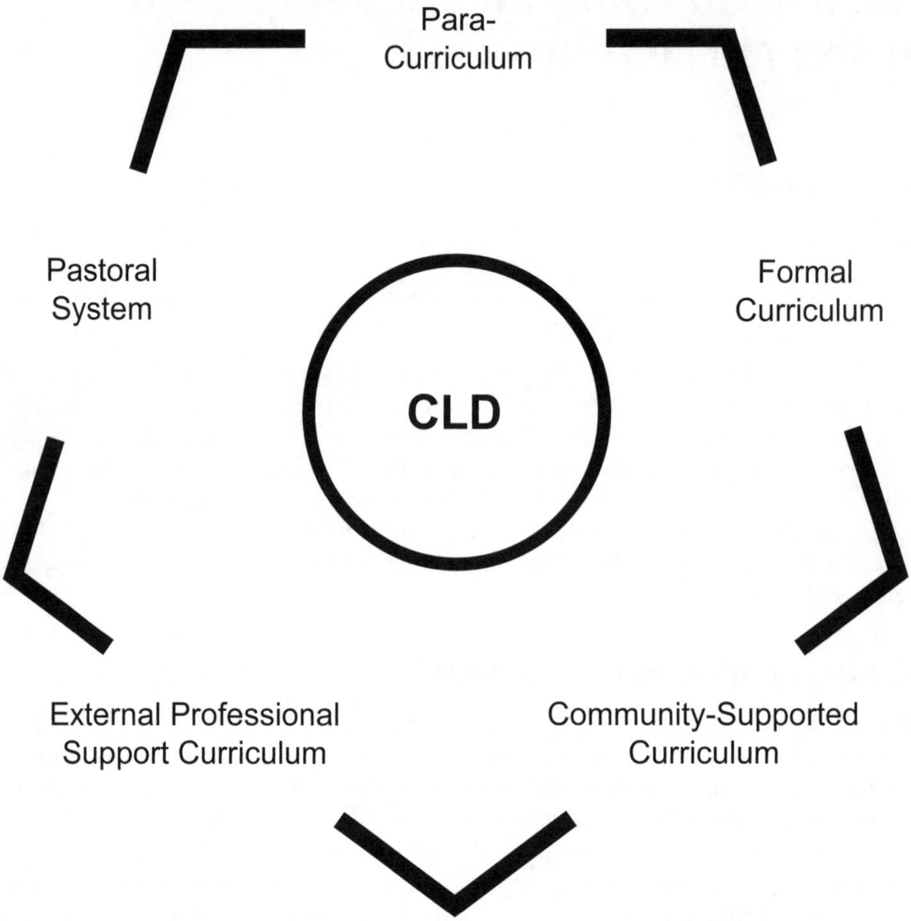

Figure 5.1 CLD curriculum structures

trate their contributions. However, you will know that unlike an orderly concert hall, the performance is taking place in a noisy street filled with competing priorities and changing conditions! We will now consider the potential contribution of each part to young people's career learning and development.

Para-curriculum

The para-curriculum includes the 'hidden curriculum' that is transmitted both implicitly and explicitly through the ethos and shared values of the school. Assemblies, school routines and ceremonial occasions such as prize days are important vehicles for this. School value systems are often strongly supportive of CLD especially when they focus on values such as excellence, aspiration, enterprise, self-efficacy (a 'can-do' attitude), resilience, ambition, fairness, diversity, sustainable living, happiness, contribution and service to others. While young people often absorb these influences silently through the para-curriculum, opportunities should be found in the formal curriculum to enable young people to explore and clarify their 'career' values (Barnes 2008). Some schools are now training students to be 'career champions' in order to help build a career development culture in the school (Reason 2009).

Extra-curricular activities are a vital part of the para-curriculum that can make a significant difference to the career opportunities of young people. After-school clubs, societies, sports and performing arts activities give young people the chance to discover interests and talents often in a serendipitous way and to acquire a track record which can provide evidence of career commitment, experience and achievement. The 'extended schools' initiative in England has widened access and expanded the scope of extra-curricular activities, but CLD practitioners have been relatively slow to realise the potential of this initiative (Barnes and Chant 2008). Extra-curricular activities are suitable for delivering personalised aspects of careers education where it is not necessary for all young people to experience the same provision. As a CLD practitioner, you need to take advantage of this delivery structure – some young people will build their careers around what they do outside the formal curriculum rather than within it!

Formal curriculum

The formal or taught curriculum comprises general/academic as well as applied and vocational education. In the United States, 'career or technical education' is a recognised term for a type of education defined by the relevance of the learning to the world of work (Hoyt 2005). From this perspective, it is interesting to think of the 14–19 Diploma in England as 'career education'. The emphasis on career and labour market information in the principal learning for these sector-led diplomas and the priority given to skills development (e.g. functional and personal, learning and thinking skills), work experience and project management in the generic learning are probably what curriculum designers would incorporate if they were designing a type of education called career education from scratch!

Careers education is normally viewed in England as a 'quasi-subject' either in its own right or as part of a wider construct such as PSHEe. Traditionally, subjects have been one of the most successful ways of organising learning in schools. The case for treating careers education as 'a subject' is that it has:

- 'career' as its central organising concept supported by other big ideas (such as work, role and transition) just as other subjects have their key concepts;
- a distinctive body of knowledge centring on the understanding and skills that young people need to know themselves better, explore the world of work and build their careers;
- a focus of enquiry which is relevant to the personal, social and economic well-being of individuals, society and the economy;
- a recognised pedagogy rooted in active, interactive, participative and experiential learning approaches;
- rigorous perspectives, methods and forms of explanation rooted in humanities and social science disciplines.

Treating careers education as a subject focuses on career learning as a cognitive activity. The national support programme for careers education developed a scheme of work in which unit titles were based on enquiry questions (CESP 2004). Box 5.1 summarises the unit titles. More recently, a discussion has opened up in higher education on the potential role of 'career studies' in transforming careers education in higher education (McCash 2008, 2010).

Box 5.1 A scheme of work for careers education (CESP 2004)

Key Stage 3

1   What will I learn in CEG?
2   What am I like?
3   Why do people work?
4   How do people investigate the world of work and its opportunities?
5   How do I make best use of careers information?
6   What's involved in making decisions at 13+?
7   What is the world of work like?

Key Stage 4

8   How am I changing?
9   How can work experience help me?
10 What's involved in managing decisions and transitions at 16+?
11 How do I make effective applications?
12 How do people deal with problems at work?

Post-16

13 How do I manage my career?
14 How are careers changing?
15 How can I improve my 'career capital'?
16 What's involved in choosing FE, training or employment at 17+?
17 What's involved in choosing higher education?

However, treating career education as a subject in secondary education can also be problematic. Some young people may be put off by an overtly academic approach, and the proliferation in the number of school subjects and the strong boundaries between them can lead to fragmented learning experiences (and timetables) for young people. Competing pressures on curriculum time can also mean that the inputs are insufficient. Differences of status between subjects can affect young people's motivation and commitment, especially if careers education is perceived as a non-examined and, therefore, less important subject. Where opportunities for discrete or stand-alone career education are restricted, it makes sense to use this time for:

- urgent procedural and time-bound matters – for example, choosing options, making applications;
- 'big picture' and synthetic issues – for example, overview of the careers programme, the importance of developing career management skills.

A more challenging way forward for schools is to combine 'separate' provision with 'integrated' provision. Integrated provision can take a number of different forms. One approach is to make connections between subjects for mutual advantage. Arranging a lesson on 'careers using history', for example, helps young people to see the relevance of studying history and encourages further career exploration. Making career-related learning links to subjects can lead to deeper and richer learning experiences for young people (see Box 5.2).

Box 5.2 The potential for career-related learning in subjects

Art and design

Young people could:

- develop a visual language for expressing ideas about careers and work;
- find out about a career as an artist, craftsperson or designer;
- respond to paintings, photographs and other representations of workpeople and workplaces.

Citizenship

Young people could:

- discuss the link between different kinds of work (e.g. volunteering, 'green and sustainable careers') and active citizenship;
- discuss fairness, inclusion and diversity in relation to how career opportunities are distributed in society;
- find out about rights and responsibilities at work.

Design and Technology

Young people could:

- investigate how scientific and technological developments are transforming work environments;
- take part in a 'design and make' simulation to explore their attitudes to risk, enterprise and working for themselves;
- use creative thinking to design a new range of work clothes for a retail organisation.

English

Young people could:

- tell different versions of their own story to different audiences;
- write personal reflections on experiences that have changed their outlook on life and work;
- explore themes of career disappointment and success in novels, poems and plays.

Geography

Young people could:

- explore the geographical explanations for the labour market trends in a real place such as the area around their school;
- explore the meaning of sustainable development for people's future careers;
- use maps to interpret commuting patterns.

History

Young people could:

- investigate the impact on human lives of economic and industrial change in an identified period;
- investigate the way in which attitudes to women working have changed in Britain over time;
- critically evaluate how society uses heroes to inspire young people in thinking about their future.

Information and Communication Technology

Young people could:

- find out how to manage their online identities and networks to assist their job seeking;
- investigate the impact of ICT on work practices;
- carry out a survey online of students' careers information and advice needs.

Mathematics

Young people could:

- investigate the return on investment of entering the labour market with a graduate qualification;
- calculate the costs of making a journey to work using different forms of transport;
- explore the maths used in jobs where people solve problems of flow such as in transport and logistics.

Modern foreign languages

Young people could:

- practise applying for a job using the target language;
- find out how etiquette and work cultures vary in the countries where the target language is spoken;
- undertake a work experience placement abroad.

Music

Young people could:

- explore the role of music in strengthening the resilience of people with difficult working lives – for example, slave songs, marching tunes, punk music;
- explore the range of careers involved in staging a show at school;
- interview family and friends about their choices of music to mark rites of passage in their lives.

PE

Young people could:

- discuss how leadership and teamwork skills practised in games and sports can be applied in the workplace;

- identify ways of staying healthy, fit and stress free in their future working lives;
- investigate how people in sport and dance cope with building new careers after their playing and dancing days are over.

RE

Young people could:

- explore the religious meaning of work in the lives of people of different faiths;
- seek answers to the questions 'Who am I?' and 'Who could I possibly become?';
- consider issues of right and wrong in discussions about child labour in the UK and around the world.

Science

Young people could:

- explore the motivation and impulses of people working in science-based industries to counter stereotypes of what a scientist is;
- investigate how people use scientific methods, techniques and skills in jobs outside the science-based sector;
- find out about teamworking between scientists and technicians with different specialisms in science-based industries.

Finding the natural links between subjects not only helps to reduce timetable congestion but also enables young people to make better connections in their learning. The scope for delivering aspects of careers education through cross-curricular learning is considerable but experience in England of making the most of this approach has been patchy. The approach adopted in the first half of the 1990s was to identify careers education and guidance as one of a number of cross-curricular themes which permeated most if not all subjects and which, therefore, could be delivered through subjects. This arrangement was always structurally weak and suffered under the weight of National Curriculum prescription. In the new secondary curriculum reforms (QCA 2007), careers education was in a structurally stronger but still ambiguous position in the curriculum (subsumed within economic well-being and financial capability). Subjects are encouraged to work together to deliver a coherent and personalised curriculum based on thematic learning for part of the time. This has been made easier by developing a common language to describe subjects, skills (personal, learning and thinking skills and functional skills) and cross-curriculum dimensions in order to facilitate collaboration between subjects. Cross-curriculum dimensions are just one of the possible 'hooks' for planning cross-curricular learning. Box 5.3 offers an example for Key Stage 3 of how aspects of careers education could be delivered through a theme linked to the 'identity and cultural diversity' cross-curriculum dimension. Making good connections between subjects and other cross-curriculum themes creates scope for unifying and deepening learning and exploring contemporary issues in careers and work.

The core activities in CLD that can be delivered in discrete or separate curriculum time, or through a combination of the two, need to be based on 'powerful approaches' that promote deep and compelling learning. Box 5.4 illustrates powerful approaches in CLD.

Box 5.3 Cross-curriculum dimensions: career-related thematic learning example

Thematic learning example

Working together

Cross-curriculum dimension

Identity and cultural diversity

Potential lines of enquiry (careers)

- Why is teamwork so important to organisations?
- What is the business case for having an ethnically diverse workforce?
- How can organisations build a cohesive and united workforce?
- What skills and code of ethics do employees need to promote equality and respect for diversity?

Opportunities for subjects to be involved

PE, RE, citizenship, PSHEe, ICT, English

Compelling learning experience

Interview staff from local companies and produce a report on the effectiveness of their strategies to promote 'working together'

Box 5.4 'Powerful approaches' in career learning and development

- Self-awareness activities that enable young people to assess their own qualities, skills, interests, attitudes and values. The benefit is increased when these activities are part of an overall approach to personal development planning, review, reflection and portfolio-building that enable young people to establish their own narratives.
- Young person-led enquiries and investigations into the world of work and its opportunities. Extended explorations promote deep, personalised and immersive learning and develop young people's problem-solving and transferable skills.
- Career and work-related learning experiences that bring young people into direct contact with people from the world of work both in and out of school; for example, work experience and mentoring.
- Games, simulations and role plays that are challenging, competitive and fun.
- Activities that strengthen young people's coping skills so that they are better prepared for transitions and moves such as help with making applications, financial planning and dealing with anxiety.
- Direct-focused teaching providing young people with opportunities to research and evaluate careers information from a wide range of resources, including online and interactive materials.

Pastoral system

As well as through the formal and para-curriculum, the scope exists for organising elements of CLD provision through the pastoral system. Schools and colleges have different arrangements in place including personal tutors (with horizontal and vertical tutor groups), super tutors, teacher-tutors, learning mentors, heads of year/year managers and heads of house. No one system is ideal – all have their advantages and drawbacks that have to be carefully managed.

In some schools, personal tutors have a more restricted role focusing on administrative matters and general welfare and support issues. Tutors with an expanded role can make a real difference to the lives of young people by helping them to plan and manage their own learning and choices. CLD portfolios can provide a powerful learning environment for young people to plan and reflect on their learning and development with the support of tutors and parents/carers. The evaluation of *Progress File* (Hall and Powney 2003), a national planning and recording of achievement system, showed that portfolio processes can have a positive impact on young people's learning, motivation and self-reliance. The expansion of ICT has facilitated the development of a number of e-portfolio products such as the Careers Wales e-Progress File: https://www2.careerswales.com/progressfile/default.asp. Ofsted (2002) noted that the role of the tutor was critical to the success of young people's use of *Progress File* and, previously, the DCSF was committed to ensuring that every young person had their own personal tutor by 2010.

The role of the personal tutor is a demanding but potentially rewarding one. Waterhouse describes it as

> the intensive support given to learners, usually in small groups, which is designed to enhance the quality of their learning. It recognises that learning is a subjective matter and so its role is to nurture, to encourage and to minister to processes that are already going on within each student. Its repertoire of skills and techniques is a broad one, drawing on the best techniques in teaching and counselling. Its long-term goal is the autonomy of the learner.
>
> (1991: 8)

In this expanded role, tutors proactively support and involve young people in managing and personalising their learning and development using a range of strategies including individual learning planning, assessment, target-setting, reflection, reviewing and reporting.

Professional support

Partnership working between learning providers (e.g. schools, colleges and training providers) and specialist external agencies (e.g. young people's IAG services) is a well-established feature of the British system. Careers advisers are trained to provide one-to-one and small group guidance activities with young people, and they are also trained to deliver careers education activities and to provide consultancy and advice on the CLD curriculum. In addition, the external service is also a provider of resources, contacts, training and other forms of support to schools and colleges.

You are probably aware that an effective partnership between the curriculum leader for careers and the link professional careers IAG practitioner can make a big difference to outcomes for young people, especially for those with multiple needs and difficulties. This focus on helping young people who are at risk of becoming disengaged and, therefore NEET (not in employment, education or training) has been a national priority for external services in the last ten years. It has led to concerns that young people 'in the middle' are not getting the help they need.

Community support

According to an African proverb, 'it takes a whole village to raise a child'. The final part of the structure that supports young people's CLD is the help that comes from parents and carers, employers, trade unions and people working in community organisations. It is an essential counterpart to school or college-based interventions.

Community support takes place in a wide range of settings including the workplace; but it can happen in schools and colleges by inviting visitors to work with students in a range of ways; for example, giving talks, running simulations, mentoring and coaching.

While some community interventions are ad hoc and unmediated, curriculum leaders for careers can organise community support along more formal lines by developing their own strategies for engaging with employers and education-business link organisations. Many employers prefer formal approaches from the education sector as it helps them to organise their support more efficiently.

Curriculum planning for CLD

We have already seen that the school has a choice of curriculum delivery structures for meeting the career needs, interests and aspirations of young people. Within the policy context in which the school operates, the school makes decisions about where career learning is located, how it is connected, what pedagogy is appropriate and how well it is resourced across these different delivery structures. If schools make little use of their scope for action, the careers programme may have limited impact, but a well-designed, planned and innovative curriculum for CLD can make a significant difference to the lives and prospects of young people.

The Qualifications and Curriculum Development Agency has developed a seven-step process for innovative curriculum development (see Figure 5.2) which can be applied to small-scale as well as large-scale curriculum development (QCDA 2008). It is intended to help schools implement the new secondary curriculum in England with its focus on designing 'compelling learning experiences' for young people. We will explore its potential here as a model for systematic curriculum planning to enhance careers education as an integral part of the whole curriculum.

Step one: Identify your priorities. From a careers perspective, step one is about 'What priorities for career learning and development can the school identify that will improve the engagement, motivation and commitment of young people and at the same time contribute to a more coherent curriculum for them? The school's priorities can come from different sources:

*   The aims, objectives and outcomes of careers education. These are derived from theory, research, policy and practice and are usually embedded in relevant national frameworks such as the programmes of study for economic well-being and financial capability at Key Stages 3 and 4 in England (QCA 2007). This framework embodies the key concepts, processes, range, content and opportunities to bring career learning to life and link it up with other parts of the curriculum.

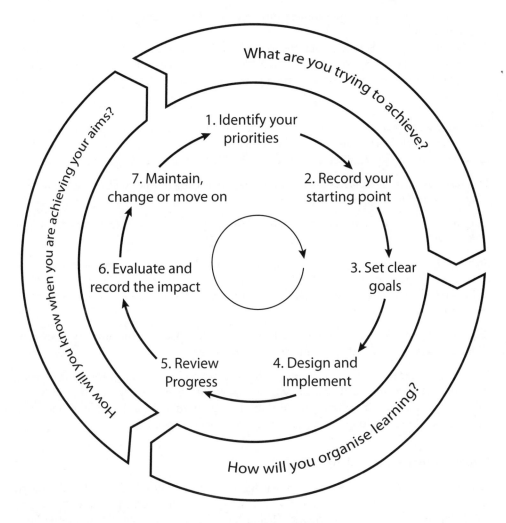

Figure 5.2 Disciplined curriculum innovation (QCA 2008)

- The career learning and development needs of young people in general and the specific needs of the school's young people. In Erikson's eight stages of development (1950), adolescence is the phase when young people attempt to find their own adult identity. The school will be aware of additional priorities relating to the abilities and socio-economic circumstances of their students.
- Educational policies and initiatives. National, local and institutional priorities have to be considered when designing the careers education programme. How, for example, should the school respond to initiatives such as the drive to encourage more young people to take up science, technology, engineering and maths ('STEM') subjects and careers, to be more enterprising or to take modern foreign languages? Specialist schools will have a particular mission which will influence their curriculum. The QCA (now QCDA) model of the new secondary curriculum envisages that subject areas will collaborate to deliver cross-curricular learning events using a common language of

skills and cross-curriculum dimensions to ensure focused and disciplined curriculum innovation.

- Specific triggers. Serendipitous events such as the opening of a new company in the area, a breaking news story or feedback from learners may indicate a priority need or opportunity. For some schools, a priority will be to award a CLD qualification to their students.

Step two: Record your starting point. Schools record what learners are like now so that they will be better able to evaluate the impact of their new priorities. The key question is 'What careers behaviour do you observe in learners now?'

Step three: Set clear goals. These will define what your learners will be like when you have achieved your priorities.

Step four: Design and implement. This step is about preparing and providing the curriculum changes to help you achieve your goals.

Step five: Review progress. Progress reviews will help you know when you are achieving your aims. For large-scale curriculum development, repeated progress reviews may be necessary to help refine the implementation plan if necessary. Chapter 9 suggests tools that you can use to support the review process.

Step six: Evaluate and record the impact. This step involves assessing the difference between where learners are now and where they were at step two.

Step seven: Maintain, change or move on. This step is about deciding in the light of your evaluation whether you need to maintain your approach, change the approach or move on to your next priority. Either way, you need to give careful thought to how you re-motivate staff who will be involved in the curriculum development.

Curriculum leadership for CLD

Schools need to consider how best to manage their careers provision to achieve synergy and coherence between the different curriculum delivery structures. In Chapter 4, we discussed the dangers of careers provision being 'everybody's and nobody's responsibility'. The expectation of the DCSF (2009) was that a member of the senior leadership team will be nominated to lead on careers. Unfortunately, every government initiative comes with the recommendation that it should be placed at the centre of the school's agenda and be coordinated by a senior leader! However, it is difficult to imagine how strategic issues related to the curriculum and external partnerships can be managed effectively without someone who functions at this level. The senior leader may in turn devolve some responsibilities but the key issue here is how to ensure that the school has leaders in place who understand how the curriculum and the organisation work and know how to plan and develop their school's careers provision.

Curriculum planning is at best a pragmatically rational process. The reality behind the systematic approach to planning the careers programme outlined in this chapter is the politics, bureaucracy and subjectivity found in school organisations that can thwart the best laid plans. Nevertheless, the curriculum leader for careers can adopt a range of approaches to improve the effectiveness of curriculum planning and development:

1   Keep in mind the principles of curriculum planning. Will the proposals for CLD strengthen personalisation and make a real difference to the learner? Will the new provision ensure coherence, continuity and progression? Will the provision promote equality and diversity? How will you ensure consistency in the delivery of the programme across the school and/or across the consortium to which the school belongs? How will you make strong connections with other aspects of PSHEe?

2   Prepare for significant curriculum development by obtaining the backing of the headteacher and the senior leadership team for what you would like to do. Box 5.5 illustrates a development and consultation process for a curriculum working party.

Box 5.5 A consultative curriculum development process

(i) Senior leadership team initiate the process outlining the procedures, timescales and expected outcomes.

(ii) A small group or working party of representative staff and school partners such as the local young people's careers/IAG service discuss ideas for the proposed curriculum development and clarify the issues on which to consult others. The group might be chaired by the senior leader with overall responsibility for career learning and development.

(iii) Consultation takes place with the larger group which could include students and parents. This could take the form of a consultation document, questionnaire or discussion meeting.

(iv) Proposals are shaped by the small group following consultation and submitted to the senior leadership team for approval.

(v) Dissemination of the policy to all those who will be affected by it is planned by senior management involving those who will be required to provide expert leadership on its implementation. Careful consideration should be given to improving the communication to parents (through the school website and prospectus, etc.) and students.

---

3   Raise awareness and create interest in the proposed developments from the staff who will be affected by them.

4   Prepare staff well for implementing the new careers provision by providing good documentation (e.g. schemes of work) and training.

5   Support staff in the early stages of implementing new curriculum plans. Try to ensure that their early experiences are positive.

6   Be aware of the pitfalls of failing to secure 'institutional commitment' to the changes. If they are just associated with a particular member of staff, they could break down if the initiator moves on.

7   Maintain your 'environmental scanning' to keep abreast of national, local and school agendas.

Disciplined curriculum innovation is an important strategy for developing and improving CLD provision. We re-visit this and discuss other strategies for strengthening CLD in the next chapter.

Discussion points

1 How can you change the perception of staff who think that careers education is just about giving information and fixing people up with jobs and training?

2 Analyse the interactions between the five parts of the CLD curriculum (see Figure 5.1) in a school known to you. How would you like to change the way that these parts work together and why?

References

Barnes, A. (2008) *Teaching about Career Values*, Godalming: CEGNET. Online: www.cegnet.co.uk/files/CEGNET0001/briefings/Teaching%20about%20career%20values.pdf (accessed 14 February 2010).

Barnes, A. and Chant, A. (2008) 'The place of guidance in the extended schools agenda – is spontaneity sufficient?', in H. Reid (ed.) *Constructing a Way Forward: Innovation in Theory and Practice for Career Guidance*, Canterbury: Canterbury Christ Church University, Centre for Career and Personal Development.

CESP (2004) *Careers Education and Guidance – A Scheme of Work for Key Stage 3, Key Stage 4 and Post 16*. Godalming: CEGNET. Online: www.cegnet.co.uk/content/default.asp?PageId=1048&sm= (accessed 14 February 2010).

DCSF (2009) *Quality, Choice and Aspiration. A Strategy for Young People's Information, Advice and Guidance*. Online: www.publications.dcsf.gov.uk/eOrderingDownload/IAG-Report-v2.pdf (accessed 12 February 2010).

Erikson, E. (1950) *Childhood and Society*, New York: Norton.

Hall, J. and Powney, J. (2003) *Progress File: An Evaluation of the Demonstration Projects*, London: DfES. Online: www.dcsf.gov.uk/research/data/uploadfiles/RR426.pdf (accessed 14 February 2010).

Hoyt, K.B. (2005) *Career Education: History and Future*, Tulsa OK: National Career Development Association.

McCash, P. (2008) *Career Studies Handbook: Career Development Learning in Practice*, York: The Higher Education Academy.

McCash, P. (2010) 'Using concept mapping to develop a curriculum for career studies', *Career Research & Development*, 23: 25–33.

Ofsted (2002) *Progress File: an Evaluation of Demonstration Projects in Schools*, London: Office for Standards in Education.

OPSI (1997) *Education Act 1997*. Online: www.opsi.gov.uk/ACTS/acts1997/ukpga_19970044_en_1 (accessed 14 February 2010).

OPSI (2003) *The Education (Extension of Careers Education) (England) Regulations 2003*. Online: www.opsi.gov.uk/si/si2003/20032645.htm (accessed 14 February 2010).

OPSI (2008) *Education and Skills Act 2008*. Online: www.opsi.gov.uk/acts/acts2008/ukpga_20080025_en_1 (accessed 14 February 2010).

OPSI (2009) *Apprenticeships, Skills, Children and Learning Act 2009*. Online: www.opsi.gov.uk/acts/acts2009/ukpga_20090022_en_1 (accessed 14 February 2010).

QCA (2007) The Secondary Curriculum. Online: http://curriculum.qca.org.uk/key-stages-3-and-4/ (accessed 14 February 2010).

QCA (2008) *Disciplined Curriculum Innovation: Making a Difference to Learners*, London: QCA.

Reason, L. (2009) *Career Champions Project 2009*. Online: www.diploma-support.org/system/files/linda%20Career%20Champions_1.doc (accessed 14 February 2010).

Waterhouse, P. (1991) *Tutoring*. Stafford: Network Educational Press.

Chapter 6

Teaching and learning

In Chapter 3, we saw the ways in which the drivers of policy for the delivery of CLD have changed over the years. As many providers are reliant upon public funding for the delivery of programmes, it is not surprising that the content of such programmes can also vary with time and with changing government priorities. However, in this chapter we consider the content of CLD programmes primarily in relation to how they meet the needs of young people themselves, without ignoring national and local priorities, cultural considerations and economic realities. But these variations need to be about emphasis and not the fundamentals of CLD. If one of the aims of CLD is to raise the aspirations and broaden the horizons of young people, academically able young people, for example, should be aware of opportunities for apprenticeships in the same way as young people from socially and educationally challenging environments should be aware of the opportunities offered by higher education.

EFFE

Our starting point is the question posed in the Introduction to this book – 'What is the purpose of CLD?' The *Statutory Guidance: Impartial Careers Education* describes careers education in the following way:

> Careers Education helps young people to develop the knowledge, confidence and skills they need to make well-informed thought-through choices and plans that enable them to progress smoothly into further learning and work, now and in the future.
>
> (DCSF 2009a: 7)

The emphasis here is on making 'well-informed thought-through choices and plans' at a time of transition. This could be interpreted as a linear process into work. However the processes involved could also be built into a longer-term decision-making model such as the CAVSE cycle (Peterson *et al.* 1996) described in Chapter 1. The description of choices as:

> well thought-through is problematic because without long-term studies how are such judgments to be made? In the short term we might judge that a reduction in the number of young people who drop out of, or fail to complete, chosen programmes of study is indicative of well thought-through choices. But longer term judgements are much more difficult to make.
>
> (Hughes and Gration 2009)

The nature and content of what we have called an essential foundation and fundamental entitlement (EFFE) is a pragmatic distillation of key elements raised by theory, policy, research and practice. In Chapters 1 and 2, we looked at some of these in some detail and they can be summarised as enabling learners to (see Figure 6.1):

- access and make effective use of impartial information and advice (IA);
- develop decision-making skills based on an understanding of 'self' and 'opportunities' (O);
- develop transition skills – for example, those involved in selection and recruitment such as interview and job search skills (T);
- reflect on self and identity in relation to their abilities, qualities and interests (S);
- challenge assumptions and stereotypes based on the seven equality strands[1] that restrict opportunities, in order to raise aspirations and broaden the horizons of young people (C);
- take charge of their own opportunities and hence futures by acquiring and developing career management skills (E).

These elements are also reflected in the *Quality Standards for Young People's Information Advice and Guidance* (DCSF 2007) and in the *Statutory Guidance: Impartial Careers Education* (DCSF 2009a).

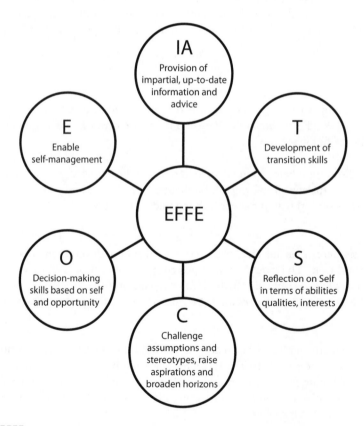

Figure 6.1 EFFE

The EFFE framework not only allows providers to reflect on the individual elements in CLD provision but also the interactions between them. For example, the provision of information is necessary but not sufficient to make an individual aware of their opportunities. Raising their aspirations could enable them to consider opportunities that they have not thought of before, perhaps because they are non-traditional. Focusing on the elements provides the essential building blocks of a CLD programme.

Teaching and learning approaches

A wide range of theories seek to explain how people think and learn and many excellent books have been written on this subject (e.g. Illeris 2009; Jarvis *et al.* 2003; Pritchard 2005). It is clear that people learn in different ways and this is sometimes influenced by what they are trying to learn and their preferred learning style or styles. In addition, as individuals we each learn in different ways depending on what we are trying to learn.

Teachers and other professionals involved in CLD use a variety of teaching approaches. These range from traditional didactic methods to more active, participative and experiential approaches. Teaching effectiveness is linked to choosing methods that are fit for purpose and take into account other relevant factors such as the time, resources and space available. Consider a CLD lesson on interview skills that is linked to the development of transition skills (referred to previously as 'T'). This could be taught in a numbers of ways as Table 6.1 shows.

CLD professionals need to be able make use of the full range of teaching methods to meet the different needs of learners, even if this involves them taking risks by moving outside their comfort zones.

Furthermore, thought must be given to the depth of learning we want young people to undertake. If CLD is to serve the long-term and complex needs of young people embarking upon their life journey, we need to provide them with more than superficial learning. Bloom (1984), in his taxonomy of learning, describes different levels of learning that enable the learner to use that learning in different ways and circumstances. Box 6.1 gives a list of these with some examples of CLD.

Bearing in mind that the overall aim of CLD is to enable young people to lead 'successful' independent adult lives, it is important that sessions of CLD provide a safe environment where young people can gain confidence, develop their understanding, and practise the skills

Table 6.1 Ways of teaching interview skills

Approach	Method/activity
Didactic	Teacher discusses the top ten tips of successful interviews listed on the interactive whiteboard
Group learning	Students discuss in small groups what to expect at an interview and provide feedback to the whole class
Simulation	Practice interviews with employers or admissions tutors
Role play	Practice interviews where students play the roles of employers and interviewees
Interactive	Learners search online for websites with interview tips, video clips of interviews and helplines
Experiential	Students prepare for a real interview and afterwards reflect on what happened and what they would do differently or better next time

---

Box 6.1 Hierarchy of learning levels in CLD

1   Knowledge – remembering or memorising, such as all post-16 options
2   Comprehension – interpreting and understanding knowledge, such as understanding the essential differences between these options.
3   Application – problem solving or using that understanding, such as using that understanding to make a choice.
4   Analysis – subdividing something to show how it is put together, such as understanding the process of choice so that it informs future choices.
5   Synthesis – creating a unique object or combination of ideas to form a new whole, such as planning and developing an individual's unique career pattern.
6   Evaluation – making value decisions, such as being able to reflect on this process in the past, present and future.

(Based on Bloom's Taxonomy of Learning 1984)

---

they need for the future. As we know, learning about career is difficult for young people (see Chapter 1), in particular because of its abstract nature. As a result, CLD lessons need to be practical and 'hands on' so that young people can gain first-hand experiences that help them to reflect on themselves and their futures. Didactic methods alone will not be enough and the following old Chinese proverb is always worth remembering in relation to all aspects of CLD delivery 'Tell me and I'll forget. Show me and I may remember. Involve me and I will understand.' Young people need to gain more understanding of themselves and their possible futures, so learner participation and involvement are vital to effective CLD. This can be achieved in a number of ways.

Problem-based learning

Problem-based learning is an approach used in a wide variety of teaching and learning situations, and promotes student involvement. It represents the 'Analysis' level in Bloom's taxonomy. A problem-based approach is active and task-orientated, where students work together in small groups to achieve a task or solve a problem. This approach helps students by:

- developing vital team-work and communication skills;
- fostering an independent approach to learning and development;
- encouraging them to be adaptable and to cope with change;
- encouraging them to pose questions;
- encouraging critical reasoning by asking them to make reasoned decisions that can be defended with reasons if necessary;
- enabling them to identify and deal with problems;
- developing their skills of independent learning and self-direction;
- increasing motivation.

The role of the teacher in a problem-based approach is to act as a facilitator, allowing the students the freedom to explore the problem identified from a number of different angles. The teacher can either give students a problem or problematic scenario, or can ask students themselves to identify one. The students then work in small groups to examine the problem and to work out possible solutions.

However, a problem-based approach is only effective when it is well structured and well-resourced and students know what they are expected to achieve and how to tackle things. Kreger (2005) has developed a useful seven-step model for problem-based learning:

1   Read and analyse the problem scenario – check your understanding of the problem by discussing it with your group members.
2   List what is known – write a list of everything you know about the problem situation.
3   Develop a problem statement – this should come from the analysis.
4   List what is needed – make a list of questions that need to be answered in order to solve the problem.
5   List possible actions – use the heading 'What should we do?' to list actions to be taken (e.g. visit the library, question an expert).
6   Analyse information gathered – in the light of the research you have done, you may then need to revise the problem statement.
7   Present findings – prepare a report or a presentation of your findings. Be prepared to justify your recommendations.

Here is an example of a problem-based activity in relation to employer recruitment showing how Kreger's model can be applied:

1   The group is given a detailed problem scenario; for example, a retailer is opening a large 24-hour supermarket in your area and they need to recruit a large number of staff in a range of roles, such as in sales, administration, bakery, warehouse, butchery, supervisory and management. Other details can be added regarding the area's population, the location of the store and any other relevant issues. The group checks that they have understood the scenario by discussing it.
2   The group writes a list of everything they know about the opening of the store and the problems involved; for example, the lack of appropriately qualified and skilled people in the area and problems relating to transport.
3   From this, they write a problem statement; for example, 'It will be difficult to find enough staff for the store because ...'.
4   They then make a list of questions that need to be answered in order to solve the problem; for example, how can we attract enough applicants? Or how can we attract a range of applicants?
5   They then list a number of possible actions; for example, devise a marketing and advertising strategy.
6   Having gathered more information, it may then be necessary to revise the problem statement; for example, it may be easier to recruit certain staff (sales) and more difficult to recruit others (bakers and butchers).
7   The group then presents their findings.

Personalised learning

Personalised learning is a structured and responsive approach focused on each young person's learning needs. It is designed to enable young people to be well motivated and to achieve their full potential. In his briefing on personalised learning and CEG, Barnes (2006: 3) states that programmes need to give 'sufficient emphasis to raising young people's aspirations, encouraging self-efficacy, promoting investment in learning and raising awareness of all options and pathways'. Personalised learning is about inspiring and motivating young people, developing their learning abilities and equalising learning opportunities by providing a relevant and appropriate curriculum for all learners.

However, young people clearly have different CLD needs and capabilities, so in this regard differentiation is important to ensure that all students engage with the CLD process. This is discussed later in this chapter.

Experiential learning and work experience

In many respects it is difficult for anyone to know if they want to do a particular job until they have tried it. It is also the case that increasingly employers look for more than qualifications when recruiting future employees and some experience can help a candidate 'stand out from the crowd'. The old phrase, 'I can't get a job without experience, but I can't get experience without a job' is often true, so it is important to look at some of the ways that young people can gain some experience to enable them to escape this catch-22 situation.

Many young people will undertake some kind of work experience placement in Year 10 or 11, usually one to three weeks, either in a block or over a period of time. Young people studying for 14–19 Diplomas are required to undertake ten days of placement activity as part of their programmes. The overall aim of work experience is to enable students to experience the world of work and to continue to develop their employability skills rather than a chance to try out an occupation of interest. However, many young people will be more enthusiastic about a placement if it is in an area related to their interests. Particular courses of study (e.g. medicine and dentistry) require students to undertake some work experience in their chosen field prior to their application to university.

It is important that wherever possible, work experience does not reinforce stereotypes and that young people are encouraged to participate in work experience in non-traditional areas. Otherwise 'protective channelling' (Wrench 1990) can occur, whereby young people are protected from a perceived risk by only being sent to certain employers. An example of this would be that only boys are sent to engineering companies as girls could experience gender discrimination. It is important to understand that engaging in this kind of 'protective channelling' condones, and even promotes, discriminatory practice.

For many students, work experience will be the most significant direct contact they have had with the world of work to that point and it can help them to:

*   begin to understand the skills they will need during their working lives;
*   practise their communication and team-work skills;
*   find out the skills and qualities that employers are looking for when recruiting staff;
*   develop self-confidence;
*   gain some experience of the world of work;
*   gain some experience of an area of work that they are interested in, to begin to confirm their chosen ideas (or otherwise).

Finding and organising good-quality work experience placements is time-consuming and challenging. It is clear that a positive experience can help students in the ways identified above. But equally a negative experience can have the opposite effect; for example, by undermining confidence. Because of this, it is important that both employers and students are well prepared for the placement. A good working relationship with staff from your local education–business partnership will be invaluable, and they should be able to provide you with advice and guidance on a wide range of issues such as health and safety, insurance and child protection. Some will also provide useful materials such as work experience logbooks.

To help students gain the most and learn experientially from their placements, they need to be well prepared and clear about what is expected of them, and to undertake a placement with a supportive employer who will give them feedback to help them to evaluate what they have learned. In addition, it is also important to obtain feedback from employers in order to maintain a database of those who are happy to offer placements. This will help when trying to match students to employers in the future. Figure 6.2 illustrates this process.

The Work-related Learning Guide (DCSF 2009b) provides practical information and advice for employers, schools, students and their parents. For an academic review of the scope and value of work experience, readers will find parts of *Rethinking Work Experience* (Miller *et al.*, 1991) still useful.

Informal learning

Work experience is a reminder that learning about career takes place in many different situations and circumstances within and outside the context of formal school learning. These situations can include the home and the local community, for example, through voluntary work or involvement in youth activities. Informal learning is the everyday learning that can be more compelling than formal academic learning as it trades in 'hot knowledge'. It can also include such things as self-study, distance and blended learning programmes and part-time jobs. Many young people can also benefit from contact with a mentor or coach – someone from outside school who will encourage them and support them in relation to their CLD process (see Chapter 10). Colley *et al.* (2003) remind us that elements of formal and informal learning co-exist in the same learning situation. The role of the CLD professional, therefore, is to try to understand and manage these interactions for the benefit of learners.

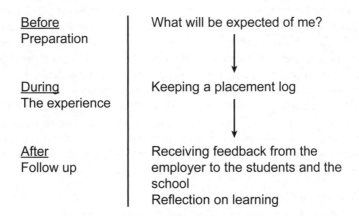

Figure 6.2 The work experience process

Planning a CLD lesson

If we think of EFFE as a strategic plan based on key elements, then the lesson plan is a 'hands-on' practical document and a framework for the lesson (Byram and Dube 2008). The principles of lesson planning for CLD are the same as for any other subject. The goals set for the lesson should be realistic but challenging. Consideration should be given to what the learners need to know in order to build on what they already know, their motivation and the dynamics of the group. Byram and Dube (2008) suggest that the elements of the lesson plan should be:

1   Engage
2   Study
3   Activate.

The Key Stage 3 strategy (DfES 2004) suggests a similar approach, which includes the use of a starter activity and introduction to the learning objectives of the lesson (Engage), the main body of the lesson (Study) and a plenary (Activate). Effective career learning should make use of as full a range of teaching methods as found in any other area of the curriculum and methods should be chosen according to their fitness for purpose, in particular in relation to meeting the needs of the learners. As discussed earlier in this chapter, didactic methods alone are not enough if all young people are to learn what they need to make informed decisions and fulfil their potential. Active, participative, reflective and experiential learning will be needed too. Now we look at the elements of the lesson plan in more detail.

Engage

A starter activity:

- gets the lesson off to a flying start;
- involves everyone and is interactive;
- focuses attention on the topic or style of the lesson or group session;
- introduces the vocabulary, atmosphere or challenges of the lesson.

This starter activity is a short 'introduction' to the session and should not last longer than ten minutes. The purpose is to create an atmosphere and energy that will feed into the rest of the session and increase the engagement of the learners. Examples include a short film or music clip followed by discussion, a quiz or questions answered in small groups or pairs, or a decision line where everyone is asked to stand on a line in a position that corresponds to their opinion or belief. The topic is then built upon in the main body of the session.

The activities or content of the main body of the session will be informed by the learning objectives for the session. These should be established by considering what the learners should know, or be able to do, by the end of the session, and should relate to your ongoing understanding of the needs of the learners. For example, you may feel that young people need to be able to compile their curriculum vitae as this is an essential transition skill. It would be important to decide when the most appropriate timing of such a session would be, to what extent the learners are aware of the need for this learning, and which specific skills and abilities should be developed. In this case, these could include:

- an understanding of the nature of a 'skill';
- a review of the skills of the individual and how and where they were developed (e.g. part-time job or interest);

- an awareness of different CV styles and formats;
- use of appropriate language.

The learning objectives should be written as 'SMART' targets: Specific, Measurable, Achievable, Realistic and Time-bound. The learning objectives might then be:

By the end of the lesson/group session each of the learners will:

- explain what a skill is;
- identify at least three skills that they currently possess and how and where they developed them;
- describe at least two different formats for a CV;
- begin producing their own CV using appropriate language and accurate spelling.

Study

When these objectives have been established, the lesson has an aim, and activities using the appropriate methods of delivery can be chosen in order to achieve that aim and meet those learning objectives. However, if the group contains a range of needs and abilities, it may be that slightly different outcomes will be achieved by some and not others. Such differentiation can be attained in other ways too. The level of support made available to some learners may be higher than for others to reach the same objectives, or different tasks could be set that are more appropriate to the abilities of some members of the group, but that achieve the same learning objectives. Such differentiation is described by Rudduck (1994: 7) as 'a classroom strategy that enables teachers to match the challenge of the task to the potential of the student'.

The purpose of differentiation is to enhance the learning and achievement of all students, to increase enjoyment and to improve behaviour and motivation; this is at the heart of all personalised learning. However, it may not be possible to have different learning objectives, tasks or levels of support for all learners in a group. A common approach would be to design learning outcomes and appropriate activities for the majority of the group, with some extension work or more advanced objectives for the most able and some additional support for those who need it, along with some alternative tasks should they be required.

The methods and techniques chosen should be appropriate to the intended learning objectives. They could include the activities shown in Table 6.2.

Activate

At the end of a lesson or group session, a plenary should be planned. The purposes of a plenary can include:

- assessment of the impact of the session on the learners;
- the drawing together of what has been learnt and whether the learning objectives of the lesson have been achieved;
- rectification of any misunderstandings;
- the highlighting of progress made on an individual and group level;
- making links to other work or subjects and to what will be done next;
- setting homework that will consolidate learning, extend it and prepare learners for future work.

Table 6.2 Activities to support specific learning outcomes

Activity	Description
Fishbowl	A small group consider a topic or subject from a range of different perspectives
Game	Problem-solving involving a team-work approach
Brainstorm	Encourages creativity and spontaneity in the generation of ideas
Card sort	Learners make decisions about grouping of topics, identifying similarities and differences
SWOT analysis	Supports analysis in terms of the Strengths, Weaknesses, Opportunities and Threats of a situation or position
Mind maps	Encourages conceptualisation of thoughts and planning of actions
Quiz	Tests to establish current knowledge or review learning
Role play	Allows the learner to reflect on experiences, feelings and realities in a safe space
Think-Pair-Share	Requires the learner to consider their own ideas and express and justify them to others
Diamond Nine	A process of prioritising which requires nine items to be put into a 1, 2, 3, 2, 1 format
Listen and Learn	A fundamental auditory learning process

In the context of the CV writing session, such a plenary might include summarising the links between the skills that the learners have identified and described in their CVs and those that might be asked for by employers. It could also include an exercise that asks students to summarise what has been covered, to write down the three most important things they will take away from the session or to make a list of things they plan to take action on that they can keep in a portfolio or file. It is worth remembering that the process of writing engages students in a deeper approach to their learning; tasks that have been written down are also less likely to be forgotten.

Assessment

Assessment can be used in a number of ways within the process of CLD. Assessment for learning, or formative assessment is designed to inform both learners and teachers of progress to date, so that the next steps can be planned. This type of learning is often most appropriate in the area of CLD. Assessment of learning, or summative assessment, is designed to inform staff and students about their achievements against specified learning objectives. Whether assessment is formative or summative, all students need constructive feedback to build their confidence and to encourage their progression, but practice in schools is inconsistent (Barnes 2009).

Portfolios and record keeping

A portfolio is a means by which students can keep a record of their learning and development. It can be used by young people to track their progress and as a place to store important documents, such as certificates, feedback on work experience placements, copies of application forms for college or university and their CV. A well-developed portfolio is a useful tool for helping students to manage their career and can be a focal point for their CLD thinking, containing records of their plans, goals and achievements.

Portfolios come in many different forms, including those that are stored on computer. Some students who progress to university will be asked to keep an e-portfolio during their course of study. Employers often ask staff to undertake courses of training and development in the workplace and portfolios are often used as part of the assessment process of work-based qualifications. In this respect, developing a CLD portfolio will be excellent preparation for future working life.

Accreditation or not?

Whether or not to accredit CLD programmes is an enduring question. The advantages and disadvantages have been summarised effectively by CEGNET (2009:1) as shown in Table 6.3.

Programmes of CLD can be accredited by a number of awarding bodies, including AQA, ASDAN, BTEC, Edexcel, NOCN and OCR. The website of the National Database of Accredited Qualifications contains information on a number of relevant courses, with useful links to other relevant websites.

Conclusion

In this chapter we have defined EFFE – the essential elements that should be made available to all young people. The ways in which EFFE is provided will vary depending on your school. In some timetables, discrete CLD can be delivered; in others, CLD will be delivered in a cross-curricular or cross-disciplinary way. In addition 'off timetable' or whole-day events may be used to supplement taught lessons. We have also discussed the importance of using a range of teaching and learning methods and how these can be integrated into a lesson plan. Finally, the ways in which learning might be assessed or even accredited have been considered. Further suggestions and ideas are contained in *Better Practice: A guide to delivering effective career learning 11–19* (Donoghue 2007).

Table 6.3 Advantages and disadvantages of accrediting CLD programmes

YES	NO
They help young people to recognise and own an important area of their learning	Young people are already over-assessed and it encourages 'credentialism'
They give young people something to aim for in their career learning	Assessment for learning is more important than assessment of learning
They help young people to prepare more effectively for entering the next stage of their learning or working lives	Young people are not motivated by qualifications that are not demanded by employers and which have a low status and currency in the real world
They provide opportunities for success, especially for young people at risk of becoming NEET or who have learning difficulties and can benefit from learning in small steps	They encourage teaching to the test and important careers topics could be marginalised
They provide evidence for the centre's evaluation of its careers provision	They are being adopted by centres to earn performance points

---

Discussion points

1   Is EFFE delivered in your institution? If so how?
2   Can you identify a range of teaching and learning methods in the way in which EFFE is achieved?
3   Are there gaps in EFFE in your institution?
4   What might be the advantages and disadvantages of accreditation of CLD in your institution?

Note

1 The UK government recognises seven equality strands: age, disability, gender, race and nationality, religion or belief, transgender identity and sexual orientation.

References

Barnes, A. (2006) *Personalised Learning and CEG*, Godalming: CEGNET. Online: www.cegnet. co.uk/content/default.asp?PageId=1067 (accessed 30 January 2010).

Barnes A. (2009) 'Assessment for Career Learning and Development: now or never?' *Career Education and Guidance*, February: 2–7.

Bloom, B.S (1984) *Taxonomy of Educational Objectives*, New York: Longman.

Bryam, H. and Dube, H. (2008) *Planning for Success: Effective Teaching and Learning Methods*, London: Continuum.

CEGNET (2009) *Careers Education Units and Qualifications for Young People*, Godalming: CEGNET. Online: www.cegnet.co.uk/files/CEGNET0001/enewsletteroct08/index.html#breifing (accessed 12 February 2010).

Colley, H., Hodkinson, P. and Malcolm, J. (2003) *Informality and Formality in Learning: A report for the Learning and Skills Research Centre*, London: LSDA. Online: https://crm.lsnlearning.org. uk/user/order.aspx?code=031492 (accessed 13 February 2010).

DCSF (2007) *Quality Standards for Young People's Information Advice and Guidance*, Nottingham: DCSF. Online: www.cegnet.co.uk/files/CEGNET0001/ManagingCEG/QualityStandardsforIAG/qual-ity_standards_young_people.pdf (accessed 3 February 2010).

DCSF (2009a) *Statutory Guidance: Impartial Careers Education*, Nottingham: DCSF. Online: http://publications.teachernet.gov.uk/eOrderingDownload/00978-2009DOM-EN.pdf (accessed 3 February 2010).

DCSF (2009b) *The Work-related Learning Guide*. Online: www.teachernet.gov.uk/_doc/13569/ The%20work-related%20learning%20guide%20second%20edition%20(final%20pdf).pdf (accessed 13 February 2010).

DfES (2004) *Key Stage 3 National Strategy, Pedagogy and Practice, Unit 5: Starters and Plenaries*, Nottingham: DfES. Online: http://publications.teachernet.gov.uk/eOrderingDownload/DfES%2 00428-2004G%20PDF.pdf (accessed 12 February 2010).

Donoghue, J. (ed.) (2007) 'Be realistic about career learning and development', in *Better Practice – a guide to delivering effective career learning 11–19*. Online: www.cegnet.co.uk/content/default. asp?PageId=2388 (accessed 13 February 2010).

Hughes, D. and Gration, G. (2009) *Literature Review of Research on the Impact of Careers and Guidance-Related Interventions*, Reading: CfBT Education Trust. Online: www.cfbt.com/ evidenceforeducation/pdf/E&I%20Synthesis_FINAL%28Web%29%20.pdf (accessed 12 February 2010).

Illeris, K. (2009) *Contemporary Theories of Learning*, Abingdon: Routledge.

Jarvis, P., Holford, J. and Griffin, C. (2003) *The Theory and Practice of Learning*, London: Kogan-Page.

Kreger, C. (2005) *PBL Model*, US: Wheeling Jesuit University. Online: www.cotf.edu/ete/pbl.html (accessed 12 February 2010)

Miller, A., Watts, A.G. and Jamieson, I. (1991) *Rethinking Work Experience*, Brighton: Falmer Press.

Peterson, G.W., Sampson, J.P.S. Jr., Reardon, R.C. and Lenz, J.G. (1996) 'A cognitive information processing approach to career problem solving and decision making', in D. Brown, L. Brooks and Associates (eds) *Career Choice and Development*, 3rd edn, San Francisco, CA: Jossey Bass.

Pritchard, A. (2005) *Ways of Learning, Learning Theories and Learning Styles in the Classroom*, London: David Fulton Publishers.

Rudduck, J. (1994) 'Enlarging the democratic promise of education', *British Educational Research Journal*, 21: 3–14.

Wrench, J. (1990) 'New vocationalism, old racism and the Careers Service', *New Community*, 16: 425–440.

Chapter 7

Challenging issues

We begin this chapter with the underpinning issues of fairness, inclusion and diversity. We will then look more closely at the needs of those young people who present with specific issues. In particular we focus on:

(A) gifted and talented students
(B) students with disabilities and/or additional needs
(C) those with complex issues.

This is not to suggest that we advocate labelling students or treating them as members of an implied homogenous group, merely that the groups above encompass a large number of students who could be described as having additional needs in relation to CLD.

Equality, fairness and policies of social inclusion – the role of CLD

'Equality', 'fairness' and 'inclusion' are terms used in everyday language that may mean different things to different people. One common misconception is that in order to achieve equality, people have to be treated in the same way. Whilst accepting that all young people should have a fundamental entitlement (EFFE), it is clear that some will need additional support.

The Equality Act 2006 aims to:

- promote understanding of the importance of equality and diversity;
- encourage good practice in relation to equality and diversity;
- promote equality of opportunity;
- promote awareness and understanding of rights under the equality enactments;
- enforce the equality enactments;
- work towards the elimination of unlawful discrimination;
- work towards the elimination of unlawful harassment.

These aims are in respect of the seven equality strands:

- age
- disability
- gender
- proposed, commenced or completed reassignment of gender (within the meaning given by section 82(1) of the Sex Discrimination Act 1975 (c. 65)

- race
- religion or belief
- sexual orientation.

Issues related to ethnicity and social background also intersect with equality issues to compound disadvantage for certain individuals and groups. The example of looked-after children illustrates how much still needs to be done. In March 2007, there were 60,000 looked-after children in public care in England (DCSF 2007). Such children and young people frequently miss out on opportunities to achieve and this inevitably has an impact on their schooling. As a result, in 2007 only 13 per cent obtained at least five GCSEs (or equivalent) at grades A*-C compared with 62 per cent of all young people.

Guidance issued to governors (DfES 2006) recommended that a designated senior teacher should have responsibility for monitoring the needs and progress of looked-after children and that all decisions about their educational options should be recorded in a personal education plan (PEP). The DCSF has developed a national strategy to strengthen support for looked-after children and new guidance was issued to schools in March 2010 (more information is available on the DCSF *Every Child Matters* website). It makes sense for careers staff to work closely with the designated teacher for looked-after children and to know about the availability of personal education allowances in their local authorities and the work of the virtual school heads who champion the education of looked-after children in the local authority.

One of the key commitments of CLD is the promotion of equality of opportunity. Evidence for this can be found in the programmes of study for citizenship and PSHEe in schools as well as in the professional training courses for those involved in CLD. In Chapter 1 we examined the work of Roberts (1997) who argues that socio-economic structures have a major influence on young people's future choices. The persistence of these barriers was confirmed in the report of the Panel on Fair Access to the Professions (Cabinet Office 2009: 6). It highlighted the worrying trend that 'the UK's professions have become more, not less, socially exclusive over time'. The government's response (HM Government 2010) proposed a new Social Mobility Commission, a new duty on public bodies to tackle socio-economic inequalities and initiatives to transform the professions and HE. It also articulated a clear role for IAG, mentoring and work experience to raise aspirations, broaden horizons and challenge stereotypes. Whilst recognising the limits of CLD-related interventions to break down the constraints of the opportunity structure, it is important that CLD professionals work in collaboration with a range of school and community partners to make as much difference as they can (see Chapter 10).

The general equality duties are framed in key legislation such as the Human Rights Act 2000, Race Relations Act 1976 and Race Relations Amendment Act 2000, Sex Discrimination Act 1975 and the Gender Equality Duty 2007 and the Disability Discrimination Act 1995 and 2005. Their provisions apply to all aspects of CEIAG. The Gender Equality Duty, for example, requires all public bodies, including schools, to tackle potential gender inequality proactively. At its most basic interpretation, this requires that both males and females are depicted in all careers information. Gender equality should be addressed proactively in the curriculum too as gender bias is established in young people long before they have access to careers information in a library (Equality Commission Northern Ireland 2002). The equalities legislation has been further strengthened in the CEIAG strategy for England which includes six statutory principles, one of which is a requirement that careers education 'actively promotes equality of opportunity and challenges stereotypes' (DCSF 2009: 49).

One example of the government's social inclusion policy is the 'Aimhigher' initiative launched in 2001. This seeks to widen the participation in higher education (up to 50 per cent of young people) by raising the awareness, aspirations and attainment of young people from under-represented groups. This initiative positively encourages participation in higher education by those who may feel that this is a choice they would not take without encouragement. This could be because they believe that higher education is 'not for people like me', or that they are unaware of the full range of their options, the support available or the potential benefits for their future. These pressures and influences are illustrative of the influence of 'cultural capital' (Bourdieu and Passeron 1973) and the cultural 'norms' that tend to reproduce themselves in subsequent generations. School-based CLD has a role, therefore, in supporting and promoting inclusion and social mobility. This can best be achieved by a 'whole-school' strategy and outlook that promotes aspiration, equality and self-determination in a committed way.

One example of the effects of such 'cultural capital' might be a family who have been in receipt of state benefits for a number of generations. A young person growing up in such a family may have very different expectations of their future than if they had the 'cultural capital' of someone from a professional family, with the expectation of a university education. Both young people may have similar levels of ability, but, without support and encouragement, their prospects are likely to be quite different.

Models of CLD delivery – the exclusive and inclusive approaches

What can we do through the provision of CLD in school to counteract the limiting effects of negative 'cultural capital'? Initiatives such as Aimhigher are one approach, but internal provision must also play its part through the curriculum. Here we will look at two contrasting philosophies for the delivery of CLD: the exclusive and inclusive approaches.

The exclusive approach

The exclusive approach provides 'equal but different' programmes for particular groups of students. This model offers different content for gifted and talented students (A) compared to that for students with disabilities and/or additional needs (B) and those with complex social issues that could present as emotional or behavioural difficulties (C). An example of this could be a programme in a school in a disadvantaged area that puts a significant emphasis on work-related learning, apprenticeships and job hunting, and pays little attention to higher education. A contrasting example would be an independent or grammar school that concentrates on university choice, the UCAS process, gap year possibilities and working in the 'professions'. In relation to issues of equality, the exclusive approach is problematic, as it could be seen to promote stereotyping and, in some cases, to lower the aspirations of young people.

The inclusive approach

The inclusive approach is about universal but differentiated provision. It begins by asserting that all young people are entitled to know about the whole range of options, and provides a generic programme for all students, which was defined as EFFE in Chapter 6. However, additional provision is also made available to acknowledge the particular needs of some students. Therefore, in an inclusive approach, gifted and talented students would be offered

EFFE plus additional work to meet their CLD needs, or EFFE + A. For a more personalised programme, it is acknowledged that any individual could need elements of more than one programme. For example a young person with learning difficulties who also has some emotional and behavioural issues may need a programme of provision encompassing EFFE + B + C.

This inclusive model reflects the current trend of educational policy to favour mainstream education for all students wherever possible with additional support as required. It also facilitates the challenging of stereotypes and can raise the aspirations of all young people.

(A) Gifted and talented students

The gifted student is currently identified as one with an overall high level of academic ability and high IQ. Many gifted students have a wide range of options available to them and require support, information and opportunities to learn and explore beyond the horizons of many of their peers.

A talented student is typically someone who excels in one or more specific areas; for example, music and/or sport. Confusion in relation to definitions could mean that a student is classified as gifted or talented in one school but not in another. Identifying gifted or talented learners is an area of some controversy. The Excellence in Cities initiative (Ofsted 2001: 12) suggested that schools target their top 5–10 per cent of pupils in terms of ability, irrespective of the overall ability profile of the school, rather than by a specific level of IQ. This, however, means that an individual may be deemed gifted in one school but not in another.

In her report on a longitudinal study of young people, Freeman (2006) questioned the benefits of labelling young people at all. In the study, some were labelled as gifted and others of similar ability were not. A third group who had random levels of ability was also followed. Freeman (2006: 384) points out that

> The group of labelled gifted were found to have significantly more emotional problems that the non-labelled group, which they mostly grew out of. Now in their forties, a gifted childhood has not always delivered outstanding adult success. Better predictive factors were hard work, emotional support and a positive, open personal outlook. By 2005, the labelled and unlabelled gifted groups are not very different in life outcomes, though both are much more successful than the random ability group.

The specific needs of gifted and talented students can be summed up as follows:

1   They recognise their potential, have their specific needs acknowledged and receive appropriate support and encouragement.
2   They understand and have access to a wide range of potential opportunities, irrespective of their background or culture.
3   Provision is appropriate and sufficient to engage and extend them, and thereby meet their needs.

What gifted and talented young people need is EFFE but with additional provision (A). This could include differentiation of outcomes by complexity, range and appropriate cognitive demand. In addition, however, a gifted young person may have quite different career learning needs to that of a specifically talented young person.

For a gifted student, their range of education and career options could be vast. Some may be particularly able in one subject (e.g. maths or science). But many very able young people find it difficult to choose between a wide range of subjects which they enjoy and in which they excel. For them the problem is decision-making, because the usual wisdom of following subjects they enjoy and are good at does nothing to focus their decisions. Their key learning need is self-awareness. They need opportunities to begin to reflect on what is important to them in their lives, so that they can harness their abilities to discover career happiness (see Chapter 11).

For the talented student the issue can be quite different. The focus of their lives may have been very sharp for some years. A talented musician or athlete will have spent many hours in practice and training every day since they were very young, and their view of themselves and of their future may be narrow and unquestioning. Careers work for some of these young people can be challenging, as sometimes decisions were made by and for them at an early age. Here the task for CLD is to broaden horizons, so that these young people are more aware of the wider world around them. In addition, they need to explore the idea that life could offer positive alternatives that could be explored. Some resistance to this is predictable, because it appears to cast doubt on their goal and even on their identity. However, this need not be the case; the reality of choosing a highly competitive path is that many will not achieve their goal, and so knowledge of some alternatives and related disciplines can be very valuable.

The focus of career guidance provision under policies of social inclusion has been on young people at risk of social exclusion, including those at risk of becoming disengaged from education. Some CLD professionals would argue that this policy has not served the gifted and talented well. The assumption is often made that the more able will have a greater degree of career maturity, but this is not always the case. Such assumptions can lead to a lack of support, resulting in misguided choices, with all the wasted time, money and effort that brings. What we describe here in (A) is a recognition of unusual potential, broad or narrowly focused. In addition to EFFE, an (A) should provide additional focus on self-awareness in the context of the adult world so that the gifted is helped to choose and the talented is allowed question choices already made.

(B) Students with disabilities or additional needs

One of the aims of CLD is to prepare young people for life choices during and after compulsory education. Preparing students who have additional needs to make these decisions will demand that particular attention is paid to their specific needs. When considering young people with disabilities or additional needs, it is important to acknowledge that these needs can cover a wide spectrum, and will require different adaptations or development of provision. These needs will, in most cases, have been identified through the process of the preparation of a Statement. It is the responsibility of the local authority to assess those needs and enable the school to respond to it.

> LEAs must identify and make a statutory assessment of those young people for whom they are responsible, who have a special educational need and who probably need a statement.
>
> (Education Act 1996, Section 321 and 323)

Section 140 of the Learning and Skills Act (2000) required all local authorities to undertake a transition plan with all young people with a Statement of Special Educational Needs (as described by section 342 of the Education Act 1996) before their final year of schooling. This Act was revised by the Education and Skills Act 2008, and these transition plans (or leaver's plans) must be written after a Section 139a assessment of the educational and training needs of the young person, and the provision needed to meet those needs. In most cases this will be undertaken at a review meeting involving a career guidance professional, the young person, their parent or carer, and other agencies as appropriate. If the young person is in a mainstream school, the review will usually include the special educational needs coordinator (SENCO). This review process can highlight the effectiveness of the programme of CLD that the young person has received and enable additional provision to be made before decisions are made about the next steps. The role of the SENCO in helping young people to overcome barriers to learning is as important in CLD as in all areas of the curriculum.

Review meetings can help to identify the range of support and provision for young people with additional needs. This includes:

- comprehensive details of courses at local FE colleges;
- details of work-based training on offer in the local area;
- information on specialist colleges and how to apply;
- information on the support available in relation to each of the above options;
- information on training allowances and benefits;
- information on help with transport to college or training;
- continued support while at college or training.

Without falling into the trap of stereotyping, it is also necessary to be mindful of some of the common outcomes for young people with disabilities; for example, that they are more likely to find themselves at the bottom of the socio-economic ladder in adulthood (Schriner 2001). Over two-thirds of disabled people are unemployed and those that are employed tend to have low earnings (Pagliano 2005). This could be the result of a variety of factors; for example, the inadequacy of anti-discriminatory legislation, poor adherence by employers to the law and failure to offer people with disabilities access to work and training, low aspirations of the individual and low self-esteem, or a combination of all of these. CLD may not be able to change legislation or adherence to it, but it has the potential to contribute to raising the aspirations and self-esteem of all young people, including those with disabilities.

Students with physical disabilities

There are a wide variety of students with physical disabilities or challenges. They include students with:

- motor disabilities
- hearing impairment
- sight impairment
- degenerative conditions, such as muscular dystrophy and cystic fibrosis.

It may be that years of professional and medical involvement have characterised the young person in terms of their disability rather than their potential: a focus on what they cannot do, rather than what they can and could do. There is a danger, and for many a reality, of parents being excessively protective and understandably cautious in their aspirations and plans for their offspring. There are also practical and financial considerations, particularly for families of the more severely disabled, that can restrict the range of training options available for the young person.

CLD as preparation for life after school is often associated with preparation for the working world. For a small number of young people preparation for paid employment may not be a likely outcome. Adult life may mean coping with other life choices such as residential care, care options at home and enjoying leisure time. CLD may be one way of trying to establish some autonomy in the lives of those for whom life has been dominated by professional interventions. In CLD this might mean a focus on recognising the choices open to the individual, however broad or narrow that might be. Decision-making requires the development of the concept of 'self' as different to others, in terms of preferences, abilities, qualities and values.

Rather than concentrating on the restrictions that particular disabilities may impose, CLD means giving students access to as broad a range of opportunities and options that focus on the possible rather than the difficult. If the student is part of a mainstream school, then this is possibly easier to achieve and as part of EFFE they will be aware of the richness and diversity of opportunities that the adult world can offer. However, they may require additional support and encouragement to pursue these opportunities and access to the practical and financial support that is available. This includes information on specialist provision such as residential care and on the available financial assistance.

In addition, practical support may be required in order to access the CLD materials and resources including:

- specialist equipment or formats such as Braille or audio delivery;
- specialist computer software – for example, word recognition.

Students with learning difficulties and disabilities

Students with learning difficulties and disabilities can range from those whose progress in school is slower than their peers to those who are unable to carry out many everyday activities that most young people take for granted. We need to recognise that just as with all those with physical or learning difficulties, there is the danger of a lack of expectation and a tendency to characterise an individual by their limitations and not by their potential. This may be one of the possible consequences of what was described earlier in this chapter as the 'exclusive' model. It is important also to draw a distinction between learning disabilities and learning difficulties. The latter are not necessarily associated with cognitive ability and may not therefore restrict career or educational opportunities in the same way. Dyslexia and dyspraxia are examples of such difficulties, which will need to be taken into account when planning CLD activities.

Many students with learning difficulties and disabilities will benefit from much of what CLD has to offer. However, it is also important to consider their potential in relation to their learning. It is useful for all young people to be aware of a wide range of opportunities, but it would be appropriate to highlight some more than others. Whatever the ability of the individual, they should be encouraged to fulfil their potential and to make their own choices whenever possible.

Additional services, provision or content for those with learning difficulties and disabilities will vary according to need but could include:

- support and advice from specialists such as educational psychologists;
- additional support or accompanying in order to attend experiences of the world of work, educational establishments or other elements of a CLD programme;
- practical 'tasters' of opportunities rather than reliance on spoken or written information;
- support from a specialist career guidance professional.

In this section, it has not been possible to include a discussion of a full range of additional needs that may be encountered by those involved in CLD such as Attention Deficit and Hyperactivity Disorder (ADHD), Obsessive Compulsive Disorder (OCD), and other conditions such as Autism or Asperger's Syndrome. In general, the severity of the disorder and the extent to which everyday life is affected will give an indication of the level of their impact on career and educational decisions. Again, however, it is important that assumptions are not made about the aspirations of the young person, but that, as far as possible, such conditions are taken as being part of who the individual is, rather than what they can or cannot do.

What we describe here as (B) is additional provision to EFFE such that barriers to learning and physical restrictions can be minimised, thereby encouraging both themselves and others to define themselves by their aspirations, not their limitations.

(C) Young people with complex issues

The final group of young people considered in this chapter are those with complex and often socially related issues. These young people may present emotional or behavioural difficulties, specific social needs or mental illness. As a result of these issues, they may also offend, misuse substances or engage in risky behaviour. Young people who are refugees or asylum seekers could also be included in the category of young people with complex issues, as they may have language difficulties and emotional and psychological issues resulting from earlier experiences or traumas. This group of young people are disproportionately represented in the NEET group and are therefore the main focus of attention of information, advice and guidance services and other professionals. Responsibility for services for these young people lies predominantly with local authorities who, in partnership with a range of agencies, should provide the services needed to re-engage them in education and training and to simultaneously reduce the number of young people in specific at risk groups. As the participation age is gradually raised to 18 (Education and Skills Act 2008), it is clear that the needs of many of these young people will have to be met in the curriculum rather than by services in the community.

Currently young people with social or emotional needs may have received little careers education in mainstream school as their attendance may have been sporadic. The career learning they have achieved may have been outside an educational setting altogether through engagement with voluntary organisations. However, these efforts can often be hampered by the young person's prevailing issues, such as lack of motivation and low self-esteem.

In many cases, the behaviour or particular needs of the young person may have necessitated a move from mainstream school to a Pupil Referral Unit, either on a temporary or permanent basis. The 'Back on Track' strategy (DCSF 2008) requires that, where such a referral is made for more than five days, an Information Passport must be written prior to the placement. This document brings together information that includes personal and family details, reasons for the transfer and relevant medical and academic information. In addition, it includes the young person's preferred learning styles, aspirations, interests and activities.

Such information will be invaluable to the development of a programme of CLD and will therefore be a vital tool for a careers professional working in such a setting.

But what can CLD realistically offer a young person with complex issues to help them to remain engaged in education or to progress into an engagement with the world of work through employment or training, thereby reducing the risk of social exclusion? The Careers Education Framework 7–19 in the *Resources Pack* for the statutory guidance on impartial careers education (DCSF 2010) offers a good starting point but can be strengthened to meet their needs in the following ways:

1   *Self-development* – a lack of accurate self-knowledge can have a detrimental effect in one of two ways. A young person might have little belief in themselves, their abilities or their prospects and so 'give up' on themselves and see their experience of education as a 'self-fulfilling prophecy'. Lack of cultural capital may have limited the possible outcomes for them, so that in their mind they see no future other than, for example living on benefits and/or outside the law, or continuing to live on the same estate with the same gang/peer group. The opposite misunderstanding can be equally destructive. A young person who has been encouraged to believe in the unattainable or unrealistic goal and has no 'back-up' plan could find it very difficult to recover from the disappointment and 'give up' on any alternatives. CLD can help learners to reflect on their qualities and skills in the context of a range of options, as well as raising awareness of influences upon them such as a need for status and fulfilling the expectations of others. CLD also helps to place the academic learning in school into the context of the adult world and thereby increases relevance and motivation.

2   *Career exploration* – young people understandably have a narrow appreciation of the whole range of opportunities available to them in education and the world of work. For some, the reality of the world of work is similarly vague and daunting, particularly if their family has little or no experience of it. Work-related learning, whether through work experience or studying for a vocational qualification can help to introduce the realities of the working world and the concept that they have a valid place within it.

3   *Career management* – the skills needed to manage a transition might be assumed for some, but for a young person who has little support from home these processes can be lacking. It is crucial then that support is readily available (not just for those who ask) on an individual basis, to encourage progression and help with such practical activities such as completing application forms, attending interviews, managing finances etc. Much of this will be addressed through individual guidance but before that point a CLD programme may need to address a fundamental skill in the management of a career – that of risk taking. A lack of confidence or self-esteem may result in an inability to make their own choices, perhaps illustrated in a tendency to follow their peers. This may result in risky behaviour which in itself appears to them to be less risky than standing out from the crowd. Making their own decisions and living with the consequences, may not be something that some will feel able to do. In order to support ownership of their choices, CLD must foster a sense of individuality, opportunity and aspiration.

Therefore, the additional provision of (C) to EFFE is primarily to promote aspiration and highlight opportunities that provide alternatives to disengagement and lack of career development. It may also include elements of (B) to meet any specific learning or physical needs. But the focus here is on supporting the young person, in order to enable them to do all they can to overcome the barriers they face.

In this chapter we have considered how CLD can contribute to meeting the needs of those young people with specific and additional needs. However, throughout we have asserted that many CLD needs are common to all young people. Personalisation, or the meeting of the diverse needs of groups of learners, should be in the form of additions to the generic programme. Rather than the mainstream of young people receiving one generic programme (EFFE), while those with additional issues receive alternatives, all young people should take part in the generic programme with those with additional needs receiving additional support as appropriate.

Discussion point

1   How well are young people with particular CLD needs supported in the school where you work?

References

Bordieu, P. and Passeron, J.-C. (1973) *Cultural Reproduction and Social Reproduction*, in R.K. Brown (ed.), *Knowledge, Education and Cultural Change*, London: Tavistock

Cabinet Office (2009) *Unleashing Aspiration: the Final Report of the Panel on Fair Access to the Professions.* Online: www.cabinetoffice.gov.uk/media/227102/fair-access.pdf (accessed 12 February 2010).

DCSF (2007) *Children Looked After in England (Including Adoption and Care Leavers) year ending 31 March 2007.* Online: www.dcsf.gov.rsgateway/DB/SFR/s000741/index.shtml (accessed 25 January 2010).

DCSF (2008) *Back on Track: A Strategy for Modernising Alternative Provision for Young People.* Online: http://publications.dcsf.gov.uk/eOrderingDownload/CM-7410.pdf (accessed 12 February 2010).

DCSF (2009) *Quality, Choice and Aspiration. A Strategy for Young People's Information, Advice and Guidance.* Online: www.publications.dcsf.gov.uk/eOrderingDownload/IAG-Report-v2.pdf (accessed 12 February 2010).

DCSF (2010) *Resources Pack to Help Schools/pupil Referral Units Implement the Statutory Guidance: Impartial careers education.* Nottingham: DCSF.

DfES (2006) *Supporting Looked After Learners A Practical Guide for School Governors*, Nottingham: DfES.

Equality Commission Northern Ireland (2002) *Betty the Builder, Neil the Nurse. Sex-typing of Occupations in Primary Schools.* Online: www.equalityni.org/sections/default.asp?secid=8&cms=Publications_Sex_research+reports&cmsid=7_39_186&id=186 (accessed 25 January 2010).

Freeman, J. (2006) 'Giftedness in the long term', *Journal for the Education of the Gifted*, 29: 384–403.

HM Government (2010) *Unleashing Aspiration: The Government's Response to the Final Report of the Panel on Fair Access to the Professions.* Online: http://interactive.bis.gov.uk/unleashingaspiration/wp-content/uploads/Unleashing-Aspiration.pdf (accessed 13 February 2010).

Ofsted (2001) *Providing for Gifted and Talented Pupils: An evaluation of Excellence in Cities and other grant-funded programmes.* Online: www.standards.dfes.gov.uk/giftedandtalented/downloads/pdf/giftedandtalented.pdf (accessed 29 June 2010).

Pagliano, P. (2005) 'The career education curriculum and students with disabilities' in B.A. Irving and B. Malik (eds.) *Critical Reflections on Career Education and Guidance*, Abingdon: RoutledgeFalmer.

Roberts, K. (1997) 'Prolonged transitions to uncertain destinations', *British Journal of Guidance and Counselling*, 25(3): 345–360.

Schriner, K. (2001) 'A disability studies perspective on employment issues and policies for disabled people', in G.L. Albrecht, K.D. Seelman and M. Bury (eds.) *Handbook of Disability Studies,* Thousand Oaks: Sage.

Legislation

Details of all equality legislation can be found on the Equality and Human Rights website. Online: www.equalityhumanrights.com (accessed 12 February 2010).

Details of all education legislation can be found on the Office of Public Sector Information's website. Online: www.opsi.gov.uk/index (accessed 12 February 2010)

Chapter 8

Staff development

This chapter considers a range of issues related to staff development: both your own development as a CLD professional and the development of those who work with you. It begins by looking at your own development and the reasons why this is important for you, your colleagues and your students. Some key aspects of the literature on reflective practice are discussed and evaluated, particularly as they relate to working in a CLD setting. This is followed by a consideration of the development of others with whom you work and the potential of teams to achieve far more than individuals within the CLD arena. The chapter concludes with a consideration of the potential impact of professional associations in the development of the whole area of CLD practice.

Developing yourself

Professionals in all spheres are expected to act with a level of autonomy and have a responsibility to take ownership of their own training and development. Working as a professional in the CLD arena is no exception to this. Even though the professional field of education has gone through changes that seemingly reduce levels of autonomy for teachers (e.g. the stipulations of the National Curriculum and strategies for assessment and examination of students), teachers and others involved in CLD need to be able to practise with a level of autonomy and to be proactive in relation to their own development. Within the CLD arena, this is particularly important when significant numbers of professionals enter it from other fields (e.g. having taught another subject before or having been involved in supporting students pastorally). In such instances, it is a mistake to assume that any experienced teacher can teach CLD. Like any other subject area, it demands relevant knowledge, understanding, skills and attitudes.

Teachers' learning

Teachers are immersed in the processes of education with their students every day of their working lives. Even so, it is easy to forget that teachers too need to be involved in learning and development, so that their practice remains creative and fresh and avoids stagnation (McGilchrist et al. 2004). However, staff development is much more than attending relevant training courses (useful as they can be) and involves a commitment to ongoing professional development. In their study of secondary school teachers and their learning, Hodkinson and Hodkinson (2004: 176) report that most teacher learning occurs through the everyday practices involved in doing the job such as learning from their own practice, observation and role modelling, collaboration with others, deliberately seeking new skills, learning from the teaching materials they use, meeting external challenges (e.g. curriculum change) and consciously looking for new creative ideas, inside and outside school. Schools and teachers can, therefore, harness these approaches to create more expansive learning environments for staff. Hodkinson and Hodkinson highlight two teachers from the same school who learn in very different ways; they have 'different dispositions to learning'. One of the teachers (Malcolm) could be described as reactive, responding to change as he felt was required by his managers. By contrast the other teacher (Steve) was much more proactive and sought out opportunities to develop himself, particularly in the areas of his practice where he felt he was weak. Malcolm tended to be isolated within his school, focusing on his own work, whereas Steve worked as part of a close team within his department, where staff collaborated on projects and shared ideas in an atmosphere of radical collegiality (Jackson *et al.* 2005). In essence, Malcolm could be described as a routine professional and Steve as an innovative professional (Weggeman 2001).

In order to fulfil your potential as a professional involved in CLD, you have a number of strategies and techniques at your disposal. These techniques are also relevant for your students as they take their first steps towards independent adult life and can be discussed usefully with them.

Reflective practice

Many experienced teachers and careers advisers will be familiar with theories of reflective practice from their initial training. Some key theoretical approaches are discussed here, in particular the ways in which they relate to those involved in CLD. One of the main goals of CLD is that students should become reflective about their own career development and there is great value when CLD professionals can model this to their students. Hence, all those involved (staff and students alike) need to engage in the CLD process.

Schön's reflection-on-action and reflection-in-action

This is the most well-known theoretical perspective on reflective practice, in which Schön (1995) discusses the shortfalls of what he calls technical rationality. From this perspective problems can be worked out using logical steps, often using a formula that has been devised beforehand. He argues that those who work in what he calls the minor professions (such as social work and teaching) cannot necessarily rely on such logical formulae, as people are individual and, therefore, different. Many of you will have heard colleagues say things such as 'I did that lesson with another group of students and it worked well, but this time, it didn't, and I don't know why.' In essence this is because people are different, and, thereby, unpredictable.

In order to work effectively with people, Schön advocates that professionals need to develop the following two aspects of reflective practice.

- *Reflection-on-action* – where professionals take time to think through aspects of their practice in order to evaluate them critically and seek improvements, to learn and tomove their practice forward. This can be done individually, with a partner or in a group. In particular, writing and discussion with others prompt a deeper level of thought and analysis.
- *Reflection-in-action* – is the kind of thinking that professionals have to undertake every day of their working lives. Because people are different and in many senses unpredict-

able, professionals working with them will need to be able to 'think on their feet', testing out different ways of working in different situations.

Schön's 'reflection-on-action' and 'reflection-in-action' form the cornerstones of reflective practice and are particularly important for CLD professionals. The CLD world is changing constantly, and those involved in it need to review their practice continually to ensure that students are prepared well for the changing demands of the labour market. In addition, students need to be able to see professionals who care about their own development and who can adapt to their changing circumstances in order to learn how to cope with change themselves. All students are in transition and need positive role models to help them engage in a reflective process in relation to their own development.

Learning styles and experiential learning

In order to engage in professional development, people involved in CLD need to continue to learn and to develop their own knowledge and skills in order to help students to develop theirs. Often this will mean maximising the learning that happens as a result of a range of experiences using 'reflection-on-action' as discussed above. Much has been written about learning styles, some of which can be helpful in designing different teaching methods to suit learners with a range of styles. However, understandably CLD professionals should be cautious about stereotyping students (or themselves) by making assumptions about them based on their preferred learning style or styles.

Honey and Mumford (2000) have carried out extensive work on the subject of learning styles and have identified the following four styles.

- *Activists.* These are doers who like to be involved in new experiences. They are often open minded and enthusiastic about new ideas. They are well motivated, enjoy making progress and can achieve a lot in a short space of time. Sometimes they act first and consider the implications afterwards; this means they can be prone to making mistakes.
- *Reflectors.* These are thinkers who like to stand back and look at a situation from different points of view. They like to collect information and think about things carefully before reaching conclusions. They enjoy observing others and will listen to their views before offering their own. This means they can be slow to act and they can also suffer from procrastination, because, from their point of view, there is rarely enough time in professional life to think things through in sufficient depth.
- *Theorists.* These enjoy critical evaluation, particularly when there is a theory or model they can apply. They think problems through in a step-by-step way and are often perfectionists who like to fit things into a framework. They are often detached and analytical rather than subjective or emotive in their thinking. This can sometimes make them appear distant and even cold. They can experience difficulties in unpredictable situations where theories and models cannot be applied and can lack flexibility.
- *Pragmatists.* These are practical people who are keen to try things out. They want concepts that can be applied to their job and are always keen to know how things will work in practice. They enjoy planning their work and looking ahead. They are less interested in things they feel they have tried before, which they feel have not worked and they can become cynical.

Each style can be seen to have strengths and weaknesses associated with it. For example, activists will often achieve a lot in a short space of time, but may rush into situations without enough forethought. Reflectors may spend such a long time thinking about things that they achieve far less. Theorists can be overly analytical and perfectionists. Pragmatists can give up easily and become cynical quickly if things do not translate into practice easily.

Overall, perhaps the key message of learning styles is that in order to maximise learning, people need to be aware of their own styles and focus on developing a strong blend of all these styles. In essence this will enable people to focus on their strengths and make improvements where they have weaknesses in order to become good all-round learners and workers.

Honey and Mumford's work on learning styles was developed from the work of Kolb (1984) on experiential learning. Kolb's cycle is now seminal in relation to professional development and learning at work and is depicted in Figure 8.1 with Honey and Mumford's learning styles attached at appropriate points on the cycle.

The four stages depicted in the cycle tend to follow from each other, shown by the arrows in Figure 8.1. In many cases (although not necessarily always) the cycle starts with 'Concrete Experience', followed by 'Reflection' on that experience. This will often be followed by 'Abstract Conceptualisation', which involves deriving general rules from the experience or applying known theories to it, and then 'Active Experimentation', which involves constructing or modifying ways of working for the next occurrence of the experience. This then leads into the next experience. All of this may happen in a matter of moments or over days, weeks or months depending on the experience. At times there may also be cycles within cycles.

Kolb argues that in order to learn the most from experience, people need to complete all four phases of the cycle, although, as someone involved in CLD, it is important to understand that this will not necessarily always happen, particularly if an individual has a strong preference for a particular learning style or styles. For example, people with a strong Activist style can often skip through the other three stages of the cycle, in order to get to the next experience as quickly as possible, thereby failing to learn from what they have done, even making mistakes again that they have made previously. Those with a strong Reflector style can spend too much time thinking about what has happened and be slow to move on to the next experience. Theorists who are interested in models may be tempted to jump into applying them in practice without sufficient preparation. Pragmatists might be so concerned with practicalities that they fail to reflect on what happened. In this respect, it is clear that those who learn most from experience are those who have a balance of all four styles.

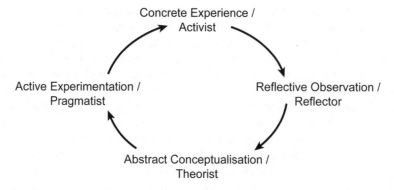

Figure 8.1 Kolb's learning cycle and Honey and Mumford's learning styles

Other perspectives on reflective practice

In his work on professional development, Eraut (1994) identifies the following three aspects of professional work, all of which are important for people involved in CLD:

- *Deliberative processes.* These are aspects of the work of a professional that require planning and evaluation. Some of the work of CLD professionals is predictable, as it tends to take place in regular annual cycles. This includes such things as the university applications process, careers fairs, work experience and visits from employers. In order for this kind of work to proceed smoothly, it needs to be well planned, organised and evaluated.
- *Skilled behaviours.* These are aspects of the work of a professional that are carried out very frequently, and which, as a result, become part of the daily routine. Over time, they require little thought and can be done almost automatically. For those involved in CLD these include communication skills, IT skills and many straightforward administrative tasks. The danger here though is that when such activities become so familiar they can become something of a 'breeding ground' for bad habits.
- *Metaprocesses.* All professionals need well-developed metaprocesses, as these are the processes that enable someone to control and direct their own behaviour and to do their work in an autonomous way. Self-evaluation is at the heart of these processes, and for those involved in CLD these are important, as in many cases they will need to operate in an independent way.

All CLD professionals must be aware of the need to work in a non-judgemental and impartial way. As young people prepare to enter the labour market, they need to be able to think about a range of opportunities and not be limited by the stereotypes that society promulgates. In particular, those young people who wish to pursue a career that is in some way outside traditional expectations, will need support and encouragement from CLD professionals. In order to give such encouragement, those professionals need to be aware of their own attitudes and values in relation to equality of opportunity and to be able to stand back and question any assumptions they may be making (Boud *et al.* 1985).

Other strategies

In this section, we present other strategies for continuing professional development that are worth considering when you are thinking about ways in which you can enhance your development.

Mentoring

The value of mentoring newly qualified teachers is well known and widely researched. You may well have experienced mentoring in this context and having an ongoing relationship with a trusted and respected mentor can be one way of helping you to develop your practice further. In relation to mentoring, the phrase 'Get One and Be One' is useful to remember, as people in all walks of life can benefit from support from experienced colleagues. In your role as a CLD professional, you are no exception to this. Your skills of facilitation and communication will also equip you to be a mentor to others including the students with whom you work.

Goal setting and action planning

These will be familiar terms to CLD professionals as they are the 'bread and butter' of work with students in career planning. Interestingly, Steve (Hodkinson and Hodkinson 2004: 174) used both strategies in order to make progress in his learning and development and he is described as 'systematic and organised in his approach to his own learning, setting himself goals and working to attain them'. At times he would deliberately take on something that he found difficult in order to address his development needs directly. This was particularly the case when he could see something that would become compulsory in the future and helped him to 'stay ahead of the game'.

In your own work, goal setting and action planning can be useful tools to help you take a focused approach to your development. Appraisal processes can help you identify the things that you would like to achieve and plan ways in which you can bring them about. Without goals it is not only easy to drift, but also to be 'done unto' by others. Goal setting and action planning can give you a stronger say in what you do.

Critical incident analysis

In any professional role that involves working with people, practice can be unpredictable as people respond differently in different situations. The work of the CLD professional is no exception to this and sometimes things will not happen in the way that you expect. The work itself is complex and sometimes situations present themselves and it is difficult to know how to proceed as there is not one single course of action that can be taken, but several. Such cases are often described as critical incidents.

The characteristics of critical incidents are as follows:

- They make you think and prompt such questions as 'What am I going to do in this situation? How am I going to respond?' (reflection-in-action).
- They prompt you to evaluate your practice afterwards – 'Did I do the right thing?' 'Could I have done better?' (reflection-on-action).
- There is not just one way of responding or a 'right' answer.
- Similar situations will not always demand similar responses.
- Often such incidents involve an emotional response and you need to engage with your feelings in order to evaluate them critically.

In such cases it is very helpful to review the work and any decisions taken. This can be done effectively with an experienced colleague or a small group where the case is examined and possible options discussed. This can be very helpful for similar scenarios that may present themselves in the future and sharpens your thinking as well as your practice.

Professional development portfolios

CLD is often about enabling students to be strategic in their career planning. This involves helping students to put themselves into the best possible position to achieve their goals. As a CLD professional, you can also benefit from taking a strategic approach to your own development. Many people find it helpful to use some kind of tool to help them map their progress, as it makes thinking about the future less abstract and can foster motivation. The Professional and Career Development Support Tool available on the TeacherNet website is one example of a tool that can help you to map progress towards your goals.

'But I don't have time to reflect or to think about my development'

Many CLD professionals (along with many professionals in other fields) often feel that they do not have time to reflect. Professional lives seem to get busier all the time, and the days of being able to get to the bottom of a 'to do list' by the end of the day seem to have gone for ever. However, it is a mistake to rush from one situation to another in an attempt to try to do as much as possible. In her book, *Time to Think*, Kline (1999) asserts that the time professionals spend thinking is time invested, as ultimately it saves time, as fewer mistakes are made and work generally becomes more satisfying. She advocates spending a short period of time (say fifteen minutes) thinking each day, which can ultimately save time and energy later on. This is a discipline that it is well worth developing.

Professional qualifications

Research for the DCSF (McCrone *et al.* 2009: 2) shows that about one-third of careers coordinators in schools have a professional qualification in careers work. The aspiration to gain a qualification was not as widespread as might have been expected, but was strongest 'amongst those coordinators who were less experienced, those who were non-teachers and those who recognised that a new qualification would help them to do their job better and would be good for professional development'. As well as recording the barriers to participation, the survey asked respondents what they would want from a new qualification. They expressed a preference for a combination of e-learning and face-to-face delivery, a mixture of compulsory and optional modules relevant to them and portfolio assessment. Barnes and Chant (2010) have argued that policy-makers and those working in the professional field need to make qualifications for careers specialists more accessible in order to help raise standards and to create a career development framework for careers specialists that is integrated with mainstream initiatives in the development of the children's and young people's workforce.

Developing others

Being involved in CLD brings numerous challenges and at the heart of the process is preparing young people for a fruitful and satisfying independent adult life, however they define it. Ultimately, everyone in schools and in education more broadly is working towards this goal and is involved in this process, therefore, in order for CLD to be as effective as possible, it needs to be delivered and facilitated by a number of people. In this sense, no one in education can say that they are not involved in careers work.

In schools and colleges, leadership needs to happen at a number of levels. Those in senior management positions have the responsibility to lead the whole institution: department heads lead in particular subject areas, year heads lead from a student welfare perspective and individual teachers lead in their classrooms. In short, leadership needs to happen at every level and is often referred to as distributed leadership (Harris 2008). All staff with management responsibilities carry out their work with teams of people, who help them achieve their objectives Those involved in CLD also have a leadership role to play in order to ensure that the curriculum and support given to students is stimulating and appropriate. In many instances they have to work with senior managers, subject specialists and pastoral staff in order to meet the needs of the students – this can be described as leading from the middle (Naylor *et al.* 2006). The National College has several useful publications for middle leaders, details of which can be found on their website (www.ncsl.org.uk/).

Teamwork

In order to deliver careers work well, teams of people need to work together to achieve positive learning outcomes for students. Such outcomes will mean that students gain greater awareness of themselves and of possible opportunities open to them, learn career management skills and gain an understanding of the need to reflect on their development in an ongoing way in order to adapt to the changing postmodern world. In relation to staff development, working as part of a well-developed team will give the opportunity for you to learn from others and to take part in giving and receiving feedback in order to improve practice in an ongoing way.

In well-developed teams, responsibilities are shared and team members work together in such a way that the strengths of team can be maximised and the weaknesses minimised. For example, in the context of CLD, some individuals will have a flair for curriculum design and planning, whilst others will have an eye for detail and a gift for thorough administration. When these two aspects come together, overall achievements will be far greater than if the individuals worked separately. In this sense, a team that performs well will always achieve more than individuals working alone.

Effective teams are characterised by interdependence, with individuals taking on certain roles (Belbin 1993) and high-performing teams are generally those where there is a good balance of roles in evidence. Belbin identified the following nine team roles and it would be useful to think about the roles that you play and other members of the teams of which you are a part:

- *Plant* – creative, imaginative and able to solve difficult problems, but may not necessarily consider small details.
- *Resource Investigator* – enthusiastic and keen to explore opportunities but may lose interest as time progresses.
- *Co-ordinator* – mature and confident but may be manipulative.
- *Shaper* – dynamic and thrives on pressure, but can be prone to upsetting people.
- *Monitor Evaluator* – sober, serious and considers things very carefully, but can lack drive.
- *Teamworker* – co-operative and mild mannered, but can be indecisive.
- *Implementer* – disciplined and reliable but can be inflexible.
- *Completer Finisher* – thorough and conscientious, but can worry too much.
- *Specialist* – is part of a team for a specific purpose, but can get bogged down in technicalities.

For example, every team needs a 'Plant' who is creative and innovative, and a 'Completer Finisher' with an eye for detail and resilience to see a project through to completion. Many of us will have had experience of teams with many 'Plants' but no 'Completer Finishers' and the consequent lack of results tells its own story. Teams that have people who can fulfil a range of roles will undoubtedly achieve more than those without. In situations where CLD is designed and delivered, it is worth considering which roles people appear to play whilst making sure that there is a good balance of roles within the team as a whole.

Another aspect worthy of consideration is the way in which teams develop over time, and Tuckman's (1965) four-stage model is particularly well known in this respect. The stages he identified are as follows:

- *Forming* – during this first stage the principal work for the team is to create a team with clear structure, goals, direction and roles, so that members begin to build trust. A good orientation process is important for this stage, so that team members quickly understand the aims and purpose of the team.
- *Storming* – this second stage is characterised by discussion (and often disagreement) about processes and procedures. As time progresses, it is often necessary to redefine aims and roles as team members try to position themselves. This stage can be uncomfortable, particularly for those who prefer to avoid conflict. However, this is necessary for the team to develop and for it to be able to perform at a later stage. If this stage is missed, difficulties and tensions will remain unresolved and can hamper the progress of the team at a later date.
- *Norming* – the third stage is where discrepancies begin to be resolved, ways of working are established and team members show a greater level of acceptance for one another. Team members feel comfortable to give and receive constructive criticism and the team as a whole becomes more productive.
- *Performing* – this final stage is characterised by interdependence, where each team member is confident in their own ability and in those of other members. Differences within the team are used to enhance performance rather than hinder it and the team makes considerable progress and achieves results.

Following this, Tuckman and Jensen (1977) identified a fifth stage (Adjourning), which can particularly be seen in the case of time bound projects. Some writers refer to this as 'Mourning', when a team needs to celebrate its achievements and disband. This can be a difficult time, particularly for high-performing teams that have been enjoyable and productive for those who have taken part.

Within the context of CLD, there are many instances where professionals and others will need to work well in teams. This could be for a specific purpose (e.g. planning a major event, such as a careers fair) or for the ongoing delivery of a range of programmes within a school or college. In many instances, new team members will need to be integrated into well developed teams, and in such instances induction is particularly important so that new members can become effective quickly. However, it is also fair to say that for some who have to work in organisations where CLD has a low profile, the idea of working in a team is a luxury. In such cases, making links with anyone in the organisation who has an interest in careers work can be helpful for future development.

Action learning sets

The focus of action learning sets is on problem-solving and in some circumstances they can be a very useful way of developing your work, in particular if you experience problems or difficulties in specific areas. Action learning is based on the relationship between reflection and action, and an action learning set is a small group of people that meets together to focus on the issues and problems those individuals bring. Each member is given time to air their views and the group helps each person to consider a range of issues in relation to the problem. Future action is then planned with the structured attention and support of the group. A major advantage of action learning is that group members are able to look at the real problems which concern them, rather than considering hypothetical ones, as they are responsible for the selection of the topic(s)/problem(s) discussed. Action learning sets function well when there is a high level of trust, friendship and support within the group and members can feel safe to express their concerns. For more on this topic, McGill and Brockbank (2004) have written a guide to action learning sets that is worth consulting.

The role of staff tutor

CLD professionals in roles such as careers coordinator often take responsibility for organising CPD activities for colleagues; for example, in after-school meetings and on in-service training days. Edwards and Barnes (1997: 103–112) suggest practical ways of designing and planning effective staff development activities for others.

Engaging with the professional community

It is important to understand that those working in CLD do not do so in isolation and in many instances there will be benefits from participating in a local, regional or national professional association (see Chapter 10). This includes a local careers association or cluster of schools, where professionals can meet to share ideas and good practice. In such settings, large-scale events (such as careers fairs and HE fairs) can be planned and the work shared between different people. This can save time and resources and in certain circumstances facilities can be shared too. Under the arrangements for Children's Trusts all schools will be part of local clusters, which gives an opportunity for a range of CLD activities to be offered to people within local communities. These clusters can bring together support staff in a variety of roles in schools and colleges. Such staff will have a range of training needs, particularly in relation to supporting children and young people at risk.

Belonging to a professional community can reduce feelings of isolation and be a source of encouragement for those who are seeking to promote change within their organisation. Sometimes local associations are organised by local career guidance services, or by local authority advisers who can offer training, advice and consultancy. Professional bodies such as the Association for Careers Education and Guidance (ACEG) and the Institute of Career Guidance (ICG) can also offer support and some HE institutions offer accredited courses for CLD professionals. It is always worth finding out about associations that operate within your area and keeping an eye open for local or national strategies that could open up possible funding for your development.

Conclusion

Programmes of CLD encourage young people to learn about themselves and their futures. As practitioners involved in CLD, it is right that you are involved in learning about your development too. By doing so you will become a role model for the young people you are working with, enabling them to see the importance place of lifelong learning in their future lives.

Discussion points

1   Take some time to think about your own development. What do you feel your development needs are and who could you discuss these with?
2   How can you reflect on your practice? Think about keeping a diary or having discussions with a colleague to help you reflect.
3   Which roles do you like to play in a team?
4   How could the local support networks that you know about promote CPD more effectively?

References

Barnes, A. and Chant, A. (2010) 'Raising the bar: from careers co-ordinator to careers leader: rethinking the training and qualifications of the main CEIAG specialist in school', in H. Reid (ed.) *The Re-emergence of Career: challenges and opportunities*, Canterbury: Centre for Career and personal Development, Canterbury Christ Church University.

Belbin, R.M. (1993) *Team Roles at Work*, Oxford: Butterworth-Heinemann.

Boud, D., Keogh, R. and Walker, D. (1985) *Reflection: Turning Experience into Learning*, London: Routledge Falmer.

Edwards, A. and Barnes, A. (1997) *Effective Careers Education and Guidance*, Stafford: Network Educational Press.

Eraut, M. (1994) *Developing Professional Knowledge and Competence*, London: Falmer Press.

Harris, A. (2008) *Distributed School Leadership: Developing Tomorrow's Leaders*, London: Routledge.

Hodkinson, P. and Hodkinson, H. (2004) 'The significance of individuals' dispositions in workplace learning: a case study of two teachers', *Journal of Education and Work*, 17: 167–182.

Honey, P. and Mumford, A. (2000) *The Learning Styles Helper's Guide*, Maidenhead: Peter Honey Publications.

Jackson, D., Temperley, J., McGrane, J. and Street, H. (2005) *Improving Schools through Collaborative Enquiry*, London: Continuum.

Kline, N. (1999) *Time to Think*, London: Cassell Illustrated.

Kolb, D. (1984) *Experiential Learning: Experience as the Source of Learning and Development*, London: Prentice-Hall.

McCrone, T., Marshall, H., White, K., Reed, F., Morris, M., Andrews, D. and Barnes, A. (2009) *Careers Coordinators in Schools*, London: DCSF. Online: www.dcsf.gov.uk/research/data/upload-files/DCSF-RR171.pdf (accessed 13 February 2010).

McGilchrist, B., Myers, K. and Reed, J. (2004) *The Intelligent School*, 2nd edn, London: Routledge.

McGill, I. and Brockbank, A. (2004) *The Action Learning Handbook*, London: Routledge.

Naylor, P., Chrysanthi, G. and Brundett, M. (2006) 'Leading from the middle', *Management in Education*, 20: 11–16.

Schön, D. (1995) *Reflective Practitioner: How Professionals Think in Action*, Aldershot: Arena.

Tuckman, B.W. (1965) 'Development sequence in small groups' *Psychological Bulletin*, 6: 203–212.

Tuckman, B.W. and Jensen, M.C. (1977) 'Stages of small group development revisited', *Group and Organization Management*, 2: 419–427.

Weggeman, M. (2001) *Kennismanagement, inrichting en besturing van kennisintensieve organisaties*, Schiedam: Scriptum.

Chapter 9

Effectiveness and improvement

This chapter investigates the link between CLD and school effectiveness and improvement. Following this, we adapt a generic school improvement model and show how it can be used to improve and strengthen the effectiveness of CLD. We examine self-evaluation, quality assurance and inspection as three main ways of securing effectiveness and improvement in CLD. The chapter concludes with reflections on the benefits of having a CLD effectiveness and improvement strategy.

CLD and school effectiveness and improvement

Stoll and Mortimore (1995) define an effective school as one in which learners progress further than might be expected when considering the school's intake. This notion of adding value ties in with the traditional definition of effectiveness as 'doing the right thing'. Stoll and Mortimore identify eleven key factors in school effectiveness. These factors can also be used to analyse the effectiveness of CLD:

1 Participatory leadership;
2 Shared vision and goals;
3 Teamwork;
4 Well-constructed learning environment;
5 Emphasis on teaching and learning;
6 High expectations;
7 Positive reinforcement of behaviour and discipline;
8 Monitoring, review and evaluation of performance;
9 Involvement of students in managing their own learning;
10 Continuing professional development for staff;
11 Involvement of parents and community partners;

Effectiveness is about making a difference and school improvement is concerned with the year-on-year improvement in learners' progress and achievements. In practice, it is very difficult for schools to register improvement in all areas of the curriculum each year not least because of factors outside their control. The issue is further complicated by different views of what to include in making a judgement about what is an effective and an improving school. What should schools be held accountable for? Learning outcomes? Well-being outcomes? Equality and diversity outcomes? Destination outcomes, etc.? Even when the criteria have been agreed, it is difficult to determine the factors and combinations of factors that are associated with effectiveness and improvement.

School Improvement: How careers work can help (DfEE 2000) pointed to the critical role of high-quality CEIAG in helping learners to succeed by motivating them, raising their aspirations, equipping them to make decisions about their progression routes and developing their skills to manage their future learning and transitions in and beyond school. It also highlighted how such individual benefits translate into wider benefits in terms of support for the school's mission and objectives in areas such as improving attendance, reducing drop-out, tackling disaffection, promoting positive attitudes to learning and helping learners to cope with curriculum changes.

The DfEE guidance (2000) also identified key factors from the sparse research, inspection and survey evidence in England as to what kind of careers work makes this impact. They include:

- having a shared vision of the purpose of careers work and how it will contribute to school effectiveness and improvement that is actively endorsed by senior leaders;
- having structured careers programmes developed in response to student needs including additional support for particular groups such as gifted and talented students;
- providing specialist advice and support to help students apply their self-knowledge and understand the career implications of their choices and actions;
- having an integrated approach to student care and support covering all aspects of personal, learning and career development;
- enabling students to fully engage with review, target-setting, learning planning and recording achievement processes to strengthen their self-reliance;
- focusing on the early development of students' self-awareness and career exploration skills to promote successful progression and transition;
- connecting careers work with broader work-related learning and community and education-business activities such as work experience and mentoring;
- involving staff in identifying career opportunities and progression routes in their subjects and in combinations of subjects;
- engaging parents and carers;
- involving people and organisations from outside the school in careers work.

A study of thirty schools by NFER for the DfEE (Morris *et al.* 2000) concluded that there was no universal formula for explaining how to optimise the contribution of CLD to school effectiveness and improvement. Multiple strategies were likely to be more effective in promoting school improvement than reliance on a single strategy of implementing better careers work. Nevertheless, the report concluded that the impact of CEG on school effectiveness was most evident in eight out of the eleven schools that operated a 'partnership' or 'guidance community' approach. It identified the key characteristics of the approach as:

- the existence of enabling structures such as those required to support internal networking;
- senior leadership support;
- complementary working between careers professionals.

Additional characteristics included:

- the extent to which business and community partners contribute to both CEG and the wider curriculum;
- the existence of a clear vision of the role of CEG among staff;

- clear and achievable aims and objectives;
- a firm grounding in 'information' with links being made between target-setting, performance data and destinations data;
- appropriate monitoring and evaluation.

The CLD improvement cycle

The DfEE guidance (2000) referred to the need for a firm grounding in 'information'. Gathering hard data to support hunches about the impact of CLD presents a number of challenges. For this reason evidence-based decision-making lies at the heart of the CLD improvement cycle (see Figure 9.1).

The CLD improvement cycle is rooted in school self-evaluation. At its best, self-evaluation:

- is an accepted, non-threatening part of everyday practice;
- involves all stakeholders in a 'multiple lenses' rather than a 'top-down' approach;
- focuses on outcomes (and not just on activity) and is evidence based;
- is part of a plan/do/review cycle;
- is realistic, manageable and makes effective use of time and other resources.

The model focuses attention on four key phases:

1   What are we good at? In this phase, the school needs to take stock of the strengths and weaknesses of its current CLD provision.
2   What should we focus on? Balancing the pros and cons of building on particular strengths or remedying particular weakness are critical judgements in improving CLD.
3   How well are we doing? This will help schools to review whether or not they need to change direction or act to increase the rate of progress.

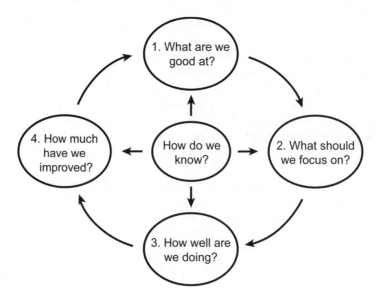

Figure 9.1 The CLD Improvement Cycle

4   How much have we improved? The final phase of the cycle involves evaluating effectiveness and improvement. It is about celebrating achievement but also about drawing conclusions and making recommendations that can be fed into the next cycle of development.

How do we know?

'How do we know?' is a pertinent question that applies to all phases of the improvement cycle. To generate management information that can be used to promote effectiveness and improvement, busy practitioners need ways of collecting and analysing data that are realistic and manageable. Useful techniques include the following.

Action research

Action research is a type of reflective enquiry which enables professionals to investigate, explain and interpret their own practice and make changes for the better. Improving CLD through action research could be undertaken by individuals or groups of professionals in a range of contexts. They may be studying together or they may belong to a school 'research and development' team.

Action research is similar to other kinds of research in that it involves systematic critical enquiry, making findings transparent and linking new knowledge to existing knowledge. However, it is unique in the way that it involves practitioners researching their own professional actions. Meeting the requirements and expectations of action research need not be off-putting even for busy practitioners if, as a result, participants are clearer about why they do what they do in CLD and what works. A number of published guides provide information and advice about conducting action research such as McNiff and Whitehead (2005) and Macintyre (2000).

The trigger points for engaging in action research are often an unclear situation (e.g. 'How effective was our careers fair?'), a difficulty (e.g. 'That group of students are very negative about their careers lessons') or an interest (e.g. 'I'd like to improve the careers library'). The first steps, therefore, are identifying an aspect of practice that you want to improve and imagining a way forward.

In preparing to carry out the research, it is a good idea to address issues of feasibility, resourcing, acceptability, relevance and priority. Involving colleagues as collaborators will help with these issues and with securing their interest in the outcomes and in making changes to their practice. It is also a good idea to identify the audiences for your research and plan at the outset how you are going to provide feedback of the findings in order to have the maximum influence on decision-makers.

The next step is to create an appropriate research design so that when you try out a new way forward, you can find out what actually happened. Deciding where to get evidence from involves issues such as deciding on the sample size – 'Is it sufficient?' and 'Is it representative?' When deciding how to gather the evidence, you need to select the method or combination of methods that will meet your purposes and remember to pilot your research instruments to ensure that they work. The most common methods of data collection are:

- Interviews and discussions – for example, 1:1 interviews, fishbowls, stories, phone surveys, focus groups.
- Observations – for example, lesson observations, sociometric charts.

- Questionnaires – for example, satisfaction surveys, suggestion boxes, graffiti boards, checklists, sentence completion, tests.
- Document reviews – for example, diaries/logs, minutes, correspondence, reports, statistics.

If your methods are flawed, you may come to false conclusions about the effectiveness of an intervention. Similarly, mistakes can be made at the stage of analysing and interpreting your findings. The crucial tests are 'Would other researchers using my data and methods come to the same conclusion?' and 'Do the participants recognise themselves in this research?' Your results will enable you to decide whether you are now satisfied with this aspect of your CLD work or whether you need to modify your practice further.

Assessment

Assessment is a way of finding out what learners know, understand and can do as a result of planned teaching and learning sessions. A distinction can be made between 'assessment of learning' which is summative and comes at the end of a period of learning and 'assessment for learning' which is formative and enables the teacher to diagnose what learners have achieved so far and what they need to learn next (see Chapter 6 for a fuller discussion).

Recording the assessment and self-assessment of CLD outcomes is essential to help those leading and managing careers work in the school to strengthen effectiveness and improvement. Recording can be carried out in a variety of ways including reports, checklists, profiles, portfolios and tracking.

Audit

Audits can vary in size, complexity and purpose. There are ready-made checklists that are easy to adapt such as the diagnostic and audit tools in the resources pack to accompany the statutory guidance on impartial careers education (DCSF 2010). The questions in an audit prompt you to take stock of the current CLD provision, rate your progress and jot down comments to help you prioritise future actions.

Baseline and benchmark data

Base lining provides a point against which improvement can be measured. Allied to this, benchmarking enables schools to compare their performance against standard measures or 'benchmarks' of best practice. Some schools compare themselves against similar schools to measure how well they are doing.

Benchmarking in relation to CLD is not well developed. A benchmarking system for CLD needs to establish and incorporate standards related to:

- Inputs and access – for example:
  - Year 9 pupils are entitled to 15 hours per year of curriculum time for careers sessions;
  - staffing levels are set at one personal/careers adviser per 500 students;
  - students have 24/7 access to an online careers portal for information and advice, etc.

- Contact and participation – for example:

  - over 70 per cent of learners in Year 10 report that they enjoyed work experience;
  - 30 per cent of the year group received one-to-one interviews, etc.

- Recorded and accredited outcomes – for example:

  - destinations known for 97 per cent of the cohort of leavers;
  - 60 per cent of pupils in Year 11 achieved a level 2 pass in the Certificate in Career planning.

Destinations data

Destinations information is collected by Local Authority Connexions/IAG services in October/November each year and published nationally. The collection and analysis of the first destinations of leavers at the school level is a useful measure of the effectiveness of the CLD programme, but the data must be set in the wider context of students' overall performance and attainment and prevailing economic conditions that are likely to affect opportunities for young people in education, training and employment. It is also important to get feedback from those who have left school about their satisfaction with the choices and transitions they have made while allowing for the fact that a proportion of leavers will have implemented temporary initial choices.

Useful ways of interrogating destinations data include the following:

- Analysing trends over time to reveal significant changes in patterns of participation.
- Taking account of any important variations in outcomes for individuals and groups of pupils – for example, boys and girls; different ethnic groups; students with special educational needs and/or disabilities; looked after children; gifted and talented students; excluded students; those taught in other institutions and groups identified by the school. Sometimes, it is necessary to look into the effects on individuals who fall within two or more of these groups.
- Analysing destinations data alongside students' overall performance and attainment to reveal significant patterns – for example, the impact of achieving level 2 passes in at least five subjects including maths and English; the progression made by students who took specific courses or combinations of subjects.

Focus groups

Focus groups are small structured groups (typically 6–10 participants) led by a moderator which meet to explore specific topics and individuals' views and experiences. You may need to hold more than one focus group to achieve a representative range of views about the aspects of the CLD provision that you are investigating. Bear in mind the comfort of the group – if it is with students, think about providing refreshments and making it easier for participants to express their own points of view. Above all, do not overrun the time they are giving you. As moderator, you need to manage the group, keep the discussion on track and be ready to prompt but avoid manipulating the group, and remain neutral. Prepare for the discussion by identifying a small number of open-ended questions, decide how to record the session and think about how you intend to 'code' the information and present the results to the school. This is a technique you can use to gauge the views of staff and parents/carers as well as students.

SWOT analysis

This is a group diagnostic technique that the team of school careers staff could use to plan improvement. The brainstorming phase is in two parts. First, the group brainstorm the 'strengths' and 'weaknesses' of the current careers provision. Then they do the same for the 'opportunities' and 'threats' in the current situation that could impact on the careers provision. When the group members move into the analytical phase, they can interrogate the results of their brainstorm in a number of ways. What are the most important strengths, weaknesses, opportunities and threats on the list? How can we build on our strengths and reduce or eliminate our weaknesses? Can we reconfigure any of the threats as opportunities? The value of the technique is in the way that it structures the discussion about what it is most important for the team to focus on.

Quality

The starting point of quality in relation to CLD provision is reliable and consistent processes that are fit for purpose. Overlaying this is the notion of excellence in the provision of CLD. Stakeholders – those that have a vested interest in the quality of provision – have a key role in defining excellence. From a careers perspective, the major stakeholders are:

- *Young people themselves.* Awareness of the importance of actively involving young people in the design, delivery and evaluation of CLD provision is one of the positive effects of the introduction of Connexions in 2001 and citizenship in the curriculum in 2004. The learner voice expressed through surveys, forums, assembly discussions and other channels is a vital way of validating the quality of CLD. Several useful resources suggest ways of actively engaging young people (e.g. CSNU 2001a, b; Futurelab 2006; LSDA 2008).
- *Parents and carers.* Surveys repeatedly show that parents and carers are the most important influence on their children's career thinking. High-quality CLD provision will be responsive to their needs. Engaging and enabling parents and carers is not only about helping them to help their own children, but also being a resource to other children in the school.
- *The school.* CLD provision impacts on learner motivation, progression, retention and achievement.
- *Employers.* As end-users of the system, employers are particularly interested in the work ethic and employability skills demonstrated by job applicants.
- *Learning providers.* The commitment to lifelong learning and the ability of young people to manage their own learning and progression are highly valued aspects of CLD provision.

The list above is not exhaustive. In a wider sense, communities and society are major stakeholders with a strong interest in the future success of the next generation. The ability of young people to secure their own livelihoods and to contribute to the well-being of others through their work are central to the meaning of 'career' and the wider social and economic benefit of high-quality CLD provision. However, meeting the high expectations of stakeholders and reconciling their competing demands is a sensitive issue for designers of quality assurance schemes.

Until now, quality in the schools sector has been managed and measured at the institutional level, but more and more schools are becoming part of federated systems as a consequence of management and ownership, specialist status or 14–19 curriculum collaboration. The challenge going forward is how to promote quality in CLD at the consortium level where under-performance by one school becomes an issue for all the partners.

Local quality standards and awards for careers education and guidance in schools are a major part of the effectiveness and improvement infrastructure. Surveys suggest that around 30 per cent of schools in England already hold or are working towards quality awards, although the figures vary from area to area. The voluntary nature of local quality awards means that there will always be some schools that never use quality assurance and accreditation as part of their improvement and effectiveness strategies. One reason for the reluctance of some schools to get involved is the cost in time and money of embarking on gaining an award; but some local authorities have introduced incentives in the form of funding and professional support to help schools achieve accreditation.

Over twenty different schemes existed in the mid-noughties. This situation differs markedly from Wales which has established a national Careers Wales Quality Award. A few of the schemes in England have achieved regional and national prominence such as *Career Mark* which was developed initially in the East Midlands and *Investor in Careers* which originated in Cornwall and Devon.

The use of local standards to measure quality and promote improvement can be problematic. The proliferation of schemes and the lack of proper evaluation of some of them brings into question whether or not they do actually measure and promote quality as they intend. This is particularly evident in the relative attention given to management issues as opposed to career impact outcomes in different schemes. One way of tackling these shortcomings could be to establish a national award or at least a national kite-marking of local awards. Quality standards in the form of guidelines for young people's information, advice and guidance were produced by the DCSF in 2007 but it is intended that they should be used by local authorities and that schools should pay attention to the six principles in the statutory guidance on impartial careers education instead (see Box 9.1). Power issues lie embedded in many quality schemes (Plant 2001) and the direction we need to travel in the future – for example, towards quality schemes that promote green and sustainable careers – still await their champions.

The rapid expansion in the 1990s of quality awards for careers education and guidance can be linked to the then current funding and accountability issues. There has always been a tension between the use of quality standards as a check on the return on investment and their use to foster the development of professional practice. From an improvement

---

Box 9.1 The six principles of impartial careers education

Impartial careers education:

1   Empowers young people to plan and manage their own futures;
2   Responds to the needs of each learner;
3   Provides comprehensive information and advice;
4   Raises aspirations;
5   Actively promotes equality of opportunity and challenges stereotypes;
6   Helps young people to progress.

(DCSF 2009)

perspective, it has always been important to stress that quality is a never-ending goal. Gaining an award is not the end of the story. In most schemes, schools are expected to submit their careers provision for re-assessment after three years and to have improved their performance in line with changes to the standards in the award scheme itself.

One of the main schemes is the *Investor in Careers* award which was developed originally in 1994. It is based on the Investor in People model and is structured around a commitment, organisation, delivery and evaluation cycle. It has been re-organised on a modular basis to make gaining the award more of an incremental process (see Box 9.2) following an independent evaluation of the scheme (Bysshe 2005).

Some of the findings of the evaluation of *Investor in Careers* have a wider application for schools thinking about gaining a quality award:

- The perceived status of CEG is higher in schools that are accredited or are seeking accreditation.
- Ofsted's assessment of CEG quality awards is generally positive, and institutions with a quality award are more likely to receive positive feedback in inspections.
- The actual benefits of achieving an award broadly match the expected benefits – for example, in improving CEG delivery.

Box 9.2 Investor in Careers: stages and main outcomes

Stage	Outcomes
Certificate of Commitment	1 School demonstrates commitment to careers education, information, advice and guidance (CEIAG) and the Investor in Careers Standard.
Intermediate Certificate	2 School has a current CEIAG policy which is consistent with statutory guidance and relevant national frameworks, contributes to whole-school aims and recognises the value of impartial information, advice and guidance.
	3 CEIAG programme is delivered to all students in the institution.
	4 CEIAG is enhanced by the work-related and enterprise curriculum through practical involvement of employers, training and FE providers.
	5 School has a written partnership agreement with local Connexions/ information, advice and guidance provider.
Full Award	6 School monitors and records students' achievements and progress, working with partners, Connexions/IAG provider, parents and carers to ensure that all students make informed choices and effective transitions.
	7 Staff involved with CEIAG are appropriately trained.
	8 Labour market and destinations information is incorporated into the CEIAG programme.
	9 CEIAG programme is systematically monitored, reviewed and evaluated to ensure that CEIAG delivered is effective in meeting the needs of all students.

- A small majority of schools that are accredited or are seeking accreditation agree that the benefits of achieving an award outweigh the costs (registration fee, staff time, etc.).
- The impact on young people in regard to improvements in their views of CEG and their capacity to make both choices and transitions is generally positive.

Inspection

Inspection provides an independent external evaluation of effectiveness and a diagnosis of what needs to be done to bring about further improvement. In conjunction with improvement planning, curriculum development (see Chapter 5), research and evaluation and quality assurance, inspection is a valuable additional tool. At the time of writing (July 2010), the Coalition government had not yet announced the changes it proposed to make to the inspection regime. Several factors influence the usefulness of inspection in strengthening CLD provision including the following.

The frequency, focus and duration of whole-school inspections

Different mechanisms may be more effective when inspections are short, infrequent and focused on other priorities besides CLD.

The evaluation schedule

The 2009 Ofsted common inspection schedule (Barnes 2010) takes into account all the factors that contribute to the school's overall effectiveness in achieving positive outcomes for pupils. It asks inspectors to reach judgements on a number of key issues related to the impact of CLD such as 'the extent to which pupils develop workplace and other skills that will contribute to their future economic well-being', 'the effectiveness of care, guidance and support', 'the effectiveness of partnerships in promoting learning and well-being' and 'the effectiveness with which the school promotes equal opportunity and tackles discrimination'. It is thus possible to use the schedule independently of inspection visits to promote improvement in CLD with the added advantage that it places improvement in CLD firmly in the context of whole-school improvement.

The inspection model

The 2009 Ofsted model incorporates moderated self-evaluation, the participation of senior staff in the inspection and active engagement of parents/carers and pupils. It is highly desirable, therefore, that staff leading on CLD think about how to use the methods of gathering evidence discussed earlier in the chapter to collect information that can form part of the school's self-evaluation data. This will include evidence to inform the judgements that inspectors are required to make as well as information about pupil destinations and compliance with careers and equalities legislation. Some of this evidence can be compiled on an annual basis and incorporated in an annual report to governors. It means that not only is the CLD provision evaluated regularly but also CLD staff are always prepared for a short-notice inspection visit.

Thematic surveys

From time to time, Ofsted carries out thematic surveys on CLD-related topics. Schools that are visited benefit from detailed feedback on their careers provision, but all schools can benefit vicariously from the findings of such surveys. Box 9.3 provides an example of a previous inspection schedule that gets to the heart of what effective CLD is about. *Moving through the System* (Ofsted 2010) looked at how well young people are supported as they move through the education system up to age 16, the effectiveness of provision to promote economic well-being and the extent to which young people are able to make well-informed choices through access to CEIAG.

Box 9.3 Unpublished inspection schedule for the Ofsted Survey of careers education and guidance in 1998

Judgements should be based on the extent to which students:

- make good progress in developing their knowledge, understanding and skills relative to their capabilities;
- know their own strengths and weaknesses, personal qualities and preferences;
- have a broad and accurate knowledge and understanding of the world of work, and of the educational, training and employment opportunities that are available locally, regionally and nationally;
- have a comprehensive and accurate knowledge of the opportunities open to themselves individually;
- are effective in making choices in relation to anticipated education, training and occupations;
- know how to manage and, where appropriate, effect transitions to new roles and situations.

Benefits of a CLD effectiveness and improvement strategy

In this chapter we have considered how the effectiveness and improvement of CLD in schools can be strengthened by active improvement planning and research, working with quality standards and harnessing inspections. Disciplined curriculum innovation (see Chapter 5) and staff development (see Chapter 8) also play their part.

The challenge for schools is how to unite these processes in a coherent strategy for ensuring the continuous development of CLD. Working out a clear strategy will help you to utilise your resources effectively. Annual self-evaluation, for example, can be supported by re-assessment for a local quality standard every three years and inspection every three to five years.

The main reason for having a strategy is to improve outcomes for young people, but it is nevertheless the case that having an effectiveness and improvement strategy may also help to raise the status of CLD in the school. If you are an unqualified careers specialist, consider leading your school's drive to attain a quality award by gaining a professional qualification in careers work. The synergy between the two will be beneficial.

There are also benefits to be had from adopting a strategic approach to CLD effectiveness and improvement at the local level. Of particular interest is the *Choices into Action* policy of the Ministry of Education and Training in Ontario (1999) which outlines the approaches that principals and teachers are expected to take when teaching students learning skills in the three areas of student, interpersonal and career development. It addresses the issues of CLD effectiveness and improvement at the system level. The way that the policy is monitored is also noteworthy. Questionnaires are distributed every three years to students, teachers, parents and community partners enabling the policy to be evaluated using a 'multiple lens' approach. A similar approach could take root in any area where schools are working in partnership with each other.

Discussion points

1   What do you think are the key factors in effective CLD provision?
2   How do you think the contribution of CLD to school effectiveness and improvement could be strengthened in the school where you work?

References

Barnes, A. (2010) *Ofsted, Self-evaluation and CEIAG*, Godalming: CEGNET. Online: www.cegnet. co.uk/files/CEGNET0001/enewsletterjan2010/files/CEIAG_Briefings_Jan2010a.pdf (accessed 14 February 2010).

Bysshe, S. (2005) *Improving the Management and Delivery of Careers Education and Guidance. Evaluation of Investor in Careers*, Derby: Centre for Guidance Studies, University of Derby. Online: www.investorincareers.org.uk/pdf/derby-evaluation.pdf (accessed 14 February 2010).

CSNU (2001a) *The Active Involvement of Young People in the Connexions Service: A Managers Guide*, Nottingham: DfES. Online: http://publications.everychildmatters.gov.uk/eOrderingDownload/1651_Managers_guide_SLATS.pdf (accessed 14 February 2010).

CSNU (2001b) *The Active Involvement of Young People in the Connexions Service: A Practitioners Guide*, Nottingham: DfES. Online: http://publications.everychildmatters.gov.uk/eOrderingDownload/1651Practitionersguide.pdf (accessed 14 February 2010).

DCSF (2007) *Quality Standards for Young People's Information Advice and Guidance*, Nottingham: DCSF. Online: www.cegnet.co.uk/files/CEGNET0001/ManagingCEG/QualityStandardsforIAG/quality_standards_young_people.pdf (accessed 3 February 2010).

DCSF (2009) *Statutory Guidance: Impartial Careers Education*, Nottingham: DCSF. Online: http://publications.teachernet.gov.uk/eOrderingDownload/00978-2009DOM-EN.pdf (accessed 3 February 2010).

DCSF (2010) *Resources Pack to help Schools/Pupil Referral Units implement the Statutory Guidance: Impartial Careers Education*, Godalming: CEGNET. Online: www.cegnet.co.uk/content/default.asp?PageId=2575 (accessed 14 February 2010).

DfEE (2000) *School Improvement: How careers work can help*, Nottingham: DfEE.

Futurelab (2006) *Learner Voice*, Bristol: Futurelab. Online: www.futurelab.org.uk/resources/documents/handbooks/learner_voice.pdf (accessed 14 February 2010).

LSDA (2008) *Developing the Learner Voice*, London: LSDA. Online: www.iagworkforce.co.uk/files/IAGXXX0001/3StrategicPlanning/3c/LSN_developing_the_%20learner_voice.pdf (accessed 14 February 2010).

Macintyre, C. (2000) *The Art of Action Research in the Classroom*, London: David Fulton Publishers.

McNiff, J. and Whitehead, J. (2005) *Action Research for Teachers: A Practical Guide*. London: David Fultun Publishers.

Morris, M., Rudd, P., Nelson, J. and Davies, D. (2000) *The Contribution of CEG to School Effectiveness in 'Partnership' Schools*, DfEE research report 198, Sheffield: DfEE.

Ofsted (2010) *Moving Through the System: Information, advice and guidance*. Online: www.ofsted.gov.uk/content/download/10961/130113/file/Moving%20through%20the%20system%20–%20information,%20advice%20and%20guidance.pdf (accessed 30 June 2010).

Ontario Ministry of Education and Training (1999) *Choices into Action: Guidance and Career Education Program Policy for Ontario Elementary and Secondary Schools*, Ontario: Ministry of Education and Training. Online: www.edu.gov.on.ca/eng/document/curricul/secondary/choices/choicee.pdf (accessed 14 February 2010).

Plant, P. (2001) *Quality in Careers Guidance*, Paris: OECD.

Stoll, L. and Mortimore, P. (1995) *School Effectiveness and School Improvement*, Viewpoint No. 2, Institute of Education, University of London.

Chapter 10

Collaborative working

In this chapter we consider the benefits of working collaboratively with a range of partners in order to enhance the delivery of CLD to young people. There have been many government documents written in recent years espousing the need for services to be 'joined up' and delivered collaboratively through partnership working; *Every Child Matters* (DfES 2003) and *Youth Matters* (DfES 2005a) and the Extended Services agenda (DfES 2005b) are just three examples. If career is seen in its broad sense ('How I am going to progress through my life course?' rather than 'What am I going to do when I leave school?'), it is clear that a number of people with varying perspectives will be involved in the CLD process. Indeed, the CLD process can benefit greatly from their involvement; a team of people is always likely to achieve more than a single individual. This chapter examines some of the ways in which these key people and services can be involved to enhance CLD for young people.

Parents and carers

To suggest that parents influence their children's career choices may seem to be stating the obvious. However, educationalists have long recognised that schools have a limited, but nonetheless significant, effect upon young people as compared to their families, communities and 'popular culture', which includes the media. The publishing of *Every Parent Matters* (DfES 2007) signalled the government's new thinking about the importance of working in partnership with parents in their children's education. Parent–school contracts are not new but this document heralded not only partnerships with parents but their potential power to influence educational policy in ensuring that their voices are heard in relation to the education of their children.

In this book we consider the preparation of young people for transition into independent adult life, so we must pay particular attention to the important influence of parents and carers on this process. This begins by ensuring that parents and carers are well informed about the options open to their children, which have almost certainly changed significantly since they themselves were at school:

> Supporting teenagers in the transition to adulthood is a distinct and unique phase of parenthood. Most parents manage this changing relationship with no major problems – using friends and family to help at times. However, parents of teenagers – and those in the pre-teen years – are increasingly saying they want some additional help in supporting their children navigate these challenging years.
>
> (Cabinet Office 2000: 38)

Information about newer aspects of the curriculum and relevant progression routes is crucial to prevent young people from being persuaded to stick to traditional routes by parents who may not understand the relevance of, for example, vocational options. However, simply offering information, in whatever way it is delivered, does not address some of the more subtle influences of parents (Vincent 1996). These influences can often be broadly categorised as stereotypical, but include a range of pressures and restrictions placed upon young people. Barriers to social mobility require more than guides, leaflets and careers information to be overcome.

1   *Gender stereotyping.* Influences on what is and is not seen as acceptable for males or females runs deep. The film *Billy Elliot* illustrated very clearly that to consider a non-stereotypical pathway in life was, and still is, a brave step for many young people. Despite years of effort to re-dress the inequalities of female earnings, gender representation in the board room, the armed services and in government, women are still under-represented in many aspects of society. Men also remain under-represented in some professions (such as primary teaching). This is clearly not only because of the influence of parents but also pressure from peers and the media.

2   *Racial stereotyping.* It is also clear that particular ethnic minorities remain under-represented in certain areas of the labour market and higher education. Whilst young people from certain ethnic groups (particularly those from the Far East) outperform many indigenous young people in education, others, in particular those who are Black African and Black Caribbean underperform and many fail to gain places in prestigious universities. Statistics in the report 'Fair Access to the Professions' (Cabinet Office 2009) showed that at the time of writing London Metropolitan University had the same number of Black African and Black Caribbean students as the twenty Russell Group universities combined.

3   *Stereotyping on the grounds of disability.* Succeeding in the labour market is also very difficult for young people with disabilities. Despite the Disability Discrimination Act, it remains very difficult for people with disabilities to gain entry to the labour market and to fulfil their potential (Lechner and Vazquez-Alvarez 2004). Those with hidden disabilities (e.g. mental health issues) often choose not to declare their condition for fear of discrimination.

4   Cultural capital, described by Bourdieu and Wacquant (1992), is an understanding of and conformity to 'what people like us do'. This could include families where the cultural capital is not to work at all but to sustain themselves on state benefits. At the other extreme it could be those for whom there is the unquestioned expectation that they will go to (a good) university and enter one of the professions. Cultural capital then includes an element of aspiration and a familiarity with certain types of work. This is echoed in Inkson's (2007) reference to the 'inheritance metaphor' of career, where young people follow people in their family, as this is familiar territory. It also relates to issues of social class, where opportunities available can be defined by social structures (see Chapter 1). The report 'Fair Access to the Professions' (Cabinet Office 2009) again shows that despite efforts over many years, middle-class parents are more likely to have children entering the professions than their working-class counterparts, irrespective of those children's abilities and potential.

5   *Values and ethics.* This relates to cultural capital and can include the work ethic within a family. It is through such influences that young people are socialised into the working world and develop an understanding of the purposes of work. For some, work is

primarily a means to earn a living, to get by or to get rich; there is no social function or element of service. For others, work is a vocation, something they choose to spend their lives doing, because it fulfils a deeper meaning for them. For others, it links with their interests and intrinsic motivation or passion. Increasingly, sustainability is an important aspect of the decision-making process (Everett 2007).

Clearly, young people can and should make choices for themselves but such decisions are likely to be influenced strongly by their parents, carers and families. As Irving (2000) points out, parents are limited to their own socio-economic context and their own life experience and so need support and 'upskilling' along with their sons and daughters, so that the influences they have are positive and supportive. Irving also argues that this might be best achieved by engaging with parents within programmes of careers education, over and above the standard and perhaps inadequate parents' evenings. Clearly parents can also have a supportive, aspirational and encouraging effect which should be acknowledged, celebrated and shared to encourage a more holistic exploration of the student's career decision-making processes. This will include an acknowledgement of parent and family influence and should, as Chope (2006) suggests, consider parents as partners in CLD.

There are several issues related to involving parents in CLD, which are summarised in Table 10.1.

Table 10.1 Issues relating to involving parents in CLD

Possible Benefits	Possible Difficulties
• Parents can provide the support (psychological, financial and practical etc.) which will enable their child to take up opportunities. • Parents have access to contacts and networks which could create opportunities not only for their own children but for other students as well. • Parents know more about the personality, qualities and skills of their children than the school, college or careers guidance professional does. • Young people really benefit in terms of confidence and self-esteem from parents who take an interest in what they are doing and in their future plans. • Parents' interest in their child's education and future is long term and not associated with short-term targets. • Parents have an understanding of the broader context of a young person's life, including family traditions and culture, religion and values.	• Parents can impose their own views on the types of opportunities that they feel are suitable for their child. • Parents who are neglectful, over-indulgent or authoritarian may not exercise their influence appropriately. • Suggesting to some parents that they should be more proactive could increase students' sense of pressure and confusion. • Parents have the right to be consulted about matters such as their child's options at 14+, but this might encourage them to make all decisions rather than encouraging their child to take some responsibility for these choices. • Parents' knowledge and experience of qualifications, education, training provision and the labour market, may be biased, limited or out of date. • Children have their own views about the relationship between their school and home lives, and this should be respected too. • Parents may unconsciously impose their own aspirations or unfulfilled dreams on their children. • Parents' ideas about what is appropriate for their child may be adversely influenced by stereotypes and prejudices.

Exploration of influences may reveal some of the less-than-helpful influences as described above. Working in partnership with parents also requires a willingness on the part of the parent to do so, willingness on the part of the young person to accept it and a commonality of goals for the young person, the parent and the professional. However beneficial it may be to engage with parents, it may not always be possible.

So if we accept that parents and carers have powerful influences upon the career trajectories of young people, and that information alone will not balance those influences, what more can be done to include parents in the CLD process?

Your local career guidance service

Working collaboratively and effectively with your local career guidance service will be a vital part of delivering high-quality CLD for young people. The following are some of the ways you can work together with your local service.

A programme of individual interviews and group work

Most local services will offer a programme of individual career guidance interviews for young people in schools and colleges. To make the most of their interviews, young people need to be well prepared, so that precious time is not wasted. This does not mean, however, that they need to know what they want to do in the future before they have the opportunity for a career guidance interview. In fact, interviews will be most useful for those who are unclear about their next steps and need some time to think things through. Sessions that help young people to think about what they are hoping to gain from their career guidance interview will be helpful.

Help with a Careers library

Some local services have staff with specialist information roles, who can be called upon to advise on designing a good careers library and keeping it up to date. This includes the use of relevant IT packages and software.

Attendance at parents' evenings

Staff from local services will be happy to attend parents' evenings on request. This can be a rare opportunity for parents and carers to talk to career guidance staff on a range of career related issues.

Support for young people who leave school and are unsure of the next step

When the time for students to leave arrives, your local service can offer vital support for young people who are unsure of their next steps. This uncertainty could be because they have not planned ahead, or because things have not happened according to plan. In particular, students who have not gained the necessary grades to gain entry to the university or course of their choice will need timely specialist advice to work their way through the UCAS clearing process quickly and effectively.

Knowledge of the local, regional and national labour market

Part of the role of the local service is to be knowledgeable about the labour market at all levels. As we have seen in Chapter 1, the labour market in the UK has undergone some dramatic changes, and out-of-date information and myths abound in this particular area. It is important that young people and teachers are informed by staff who are knowledgeable.

Knowledge of education and training opportunities

The next step for many young people is either to embark on some form of further or higher education or to take part in training. Staff from your local career guidance service will be knowledgeable about a wide range of opportunities within your local area, which will include local and regional further education colleges and organisations that provide training. This includes specialist organisations that provide programmes for young people who are experiencing difficulties entering the labour market due to a range of factors.

Knowledge of CLD programmes in other local schools

All schools have links with their local career guidance services and, as a result, staff from these services have contacts in all local schools. Your colleagues in other schools can be valuable sources of information, bringing opportunities for sharing best practice in CLD.

Building a strong working relationship with your local service is clearly very worthwhile, and in most cases this relationship will be founded on a Partnership Agreement. This agreement is made annually and is an opportunity for the service and the school or college to discuss aims and objectives for the year and to commit to a detailed plan of action to bring these about. It is important that a senior manager is involved in the process, so that the status of the Partnership Agreement is high.

Employers and trade unions

As young people move towards independent adult life, it is important that they are clear about what employers are looking for in their employees and trainees. Such information is most relevant when it comes directly from employers and training providers. Local employers themselves will often be happy to visit a school or college to talk to young people about the world of work, particularly if they are also given the opportunity to speak about their own organisation. This could form part of an organised programme of speakers, discussing different industries or professions. The Trades Union Congress (TUC) also runs a programme for schools, where speakers will deliver talks about such topics as 'your rights at work' and 'the importance of trade unionism'.

As discussed in Chapter 6, work experience is an important element of any CLD programme and many schools and colleges employ staff to organise placements for their students. Organising numbers of work experience placements is time consuming, and having an up-to-date database of employers who are prepared to offer placements is vital. Good links with your local education–business partnership will also play a key part in successfully gaining numbers of high-quality placements.

Young people will also benefit from building relationships with mentors who can give encouragement and support and act as role models. Mentors are likely to be professional people, or people working within a particular sector of the labour market. The mentoring process can be particularly helpful for young people who are at risk of being marginalised, although all young people can benefit from contact with someone who is currently working in their area of career interest. Mentoring can also play a vital part in raising young people's aspirations.

It is important to remember that many parents and former students will also be employers. Their current or previous involvement with the school or college is likely to make them sympathetic to requests for help and participation.

The partnership with business is multi-faceted. This is not just a reflection of differences in the size of business organisations, the sector they are in (public, private or mixed) or the sheer diversity of products and services they provide. As stakeholders, employers have a vested interest in helping schools to equip young people with the knowledge and skills that will make them employable. As employers recruiting locally and selling their goods and services in the local area, they may exercise their corporate social responsibility by supporting local schools. They will try to respond positively to requests for their involvement through activities such as visits, work experience and employees to come into school as advisers and mentors to young people, but will always need to put the interests of their business first. For their part, schools are often inconsistent partners of business. They may be aware of the benefits of context-based and experiential learning in all subjects and not just careers but engage employers in a haphazard way. Local education–business partnerships, as intermediary and enabling organisations, seek to formalise and rationalise link activities so that resources can be used more sustainably, the quality of links improved and extended, and challenging issues such as equality and diversity addressed in the issues undertaken. Professional bodies, trades unions, other education–business partnership organisations and voluntary groups also add to the richness of the learning opportunities that schools can access. In 2009, the Institute for Education Business Excellence (www.iebe.org.uk/) was established out of the former National Education–Business Partnership Network to promote high standards in education–business links.

Also, in recent years, much helpful guidance has been published for schools (QCA, 2008; DCSF 2009b, 2010) and employers (DCSF 2008a) on enhancing their involvement with each other and demonstrating impact (DCSF 2008b). Work-related learning at Key Stage 4 has been statutory in England since 2004, so much of the guidance has also been about improving the quality of work-related activities, especially work experience (DCSF 2007, 2008c).

School governors

An effective programme of CLD should be high on the agenda for any governing body and many will have a nominated 'link governor' for careers. Governors can be powerful allies when it comes to good levels of resources and can provide such things as a well-stocked library and a comfortable, private interviewing space and training for staff involved in CLD. Building positive relationships with key people on your governing body will be important to ensure the ongoing delivery of high-quality CLD.

All governing bodies are interested in the destinations of their students and this important statistical data is gathered annually by your local career guidance service. Working together in partnership will be important, so that as much accurate information as possible is gained in order to give an precise picture of the next steps of all students.

University admissions tutors

It is clear that many young people will want to continue to enter higher education, and collaborative working with university admissions tutors plays a key part in enabling young people to gain places at their universities of choice. It goes without saying that such tutors are knowledgeable about the UCAS process 'from the inside' and can offer help and support to students on such issues at writing a good personal statement and coping with interviews. They will also be happy to talk to students and staff about a wide range of aspects of university life, such as choosing the 'right' course, managing your budget and finding accommodation. Many will be happy to welcome people to one of their open days.

Most universities have links with schools in their locality and have staff working in school liaison departments specifically for these reasons. Such staff might work in the university's marketing department, or may work in their Aimhigher office. Aimhigher is a national campaign to widen participation in the university sector. It is well worth finding out about the Aimhigher activities in your local area, which could include visits, study opportunities and summer schools.

Colleagues in neighbouring schools

The 11–19 curriculum brings many opportunities for partnership working with neighbouring schools and colleges. One effective way for this to happen is the formation of an 'IAG forum' or 'CLD association', where all parties can meet together for discussion and debate. Such an association should ideally involve representatives of all the key partners discussed in this chapter.

A local audit

Effective collaborative working can only happen when you are clear about who your partners are in the process. There is great value in carrying out an audit of partners in your area and keeping a database of their contact details. Such an audit will be useful, particularly at key times (such as when organising events or meetings) and the results can be passed on when people leave the network.

Conclusion

In this chapter we have considered the value of collaborative working to provide comprehensive CLD programmes for young people. Working together with partners means that more can be achieved to the overall benefit of young people. This chapter concludes the second part of the book and in the next chapter we begin to look ahead towards the future for CLD.

Discussion point

1   How does your school engage in collaborative working to meet the needs of young people?

References

Bourdieu, P. and Wacquant, L.J.D. (1992) *An Invitation to Reflexive Sociology.* Cambridge: Polity Press.

Cabinet Office (2000) *Report of Policy Action Team 12: Young People,* London: Cabinet Office. Online: www.cabinetoffice.gov.uk/media/cabinetoffice/social_exclusion_task_force/assets/publications_1997_to_2006/pat_report_12.pdf (accessed 12 February 2010).

Cabinet Office (2009) *Unleashing Aspiration: The Final Report of the Panel on Fair Access to the Professions,* London: Cabinet Office. Online: www.cabinetoffice.gov.uk/media/227102/fair-access.pdf (accessed 12 February 2010).

Chope, R.C. (2006) *Family Matters: the Influence of Family on Career Decision Making,* Austin, TX: Pro-Ed.

DCSF (2007) *Building on the Best – Final report and implementation plan of the review of 14-19 Work-related Learning.* Nottingham: DCSF Publications.

DCSF (2008a) *Building Stronger Partnerships – Employers: How You Can Support Schools, Colleges, Children and Families.* Nottingham: DCSF Publications.

DCSF (2008b) *The Involvement of Business in Education: A Rapid Evidence Assessment of the Measurable Impacts.* Nottingham: DCSF Publications.

DCSF (2008c) *Quality Standard for Work Experience.* Online: www.dcsf.gov.uk/14–19/documents/Quality%20Standard%20forWork%20Experience.pdf (accessed 4 August 2010).

DCSF (2009a) *Quality, Choice and Aspiration. A Strategy for Young People's Information, Advice and Guidance.* Online: www.publications.dcsf.gov.uk/eOrderingDownload/IAG-Report-V2.pdf (accessed 12 February 2010).

DCSF (2009b) *Work-related Learning Guide,* 2nd edn. Nottingham: DCSF Publications.

DCSF (2010) *A Guide to Enterprise Education: For enterprise coordinators, teachers and leaders at schools.* Nottingham: DCSF Publications.

DfES (2003) *Every Child Matters: Change for Children,* Nottingham: DfES Publications. Online: http://publications.everychildmatters.gov.uk/eOrderingDownload/CM5860.pdf (accessed 12 February 2010)

DfES (2005a) *Youth Matters,* Nottingham: DfES Publications. Online: http://publications.dcsf.gov.uk/eOrderingDownload/Cm6629.pdf (accessed 13 February 2010).

DfES (2005b) *Extended Schools: Access to Opportunities and Services for All,* Nottingham: DfES Publications. Online: www.teachernet.gov.uk/_doc/8509/Extended-schools%20prospectus.pdf (accessed 30 January 2010).

DfES (2007) *Every Parent Matters,* Nottingham: DCSF Publications. Online: www.teachernet.gov.uk/_doc/11184/6937_DFES_Every_Parent_Matters_FINAL_PDF_as_published_130307.pdf (accessed 12 February 2010).

Everett, M. (2007) *Making a Living while making a Difference,* Gabriola Island, Canada: New Society Publishers.

Inkson, K. (2007) *Understanding Careers: the Metaphors of Working Lives,* Thousand Oaks, CA: Sage.

Irving, B.A. (2000) 'Reaching out to parents: a rationale for the development of inclusive approaches within career education and guidance' in *Career Guidance: Constructing the Future – a Global Perspective,* Stourbridge: Institute of Career Guidance.

Lechner, M. and Vazquez-Alvarez, R. (2004) *The Effect of Disability on Labour Market Outcomes in Germany: Evidence from Matching,* Rochester, NY: SSRN. Online: http://ssrn.com/abstract=511861 (accessed 30 January 2010)

QCA (2008) *Career, work-related learning and enterprise 11-19.* London: QCA.

Vincent, C. (1996) *Parents and Teachers: Power and Participation.* London: Falmer

Part C

Possibilities

Chapter 11

Careers work of the future

The subject of Part C of this book is 'possibilities' and the final two chapters focus on what careers work might look like in the future and how it might be carried out. Looking ahead is important in order to prepare for the future; however, it is not possible to gaze into some kind of metaphorical crystal ball to find out what the future holds. We have to look carefully at what is happening currently to try to identify trends for the future. This chapter focuses on CLD in the future and how people might think about the concept of career in relation to theory, policy and research. It introduces the concept of the CLD bridge and uses this throughout the chapter to illustrate the vital role that CLD has in maintaining the link between education, lifelong learning and work in its broadest sense.

Using the metaphor of the CLD bridge, the chapter explores how practitioners can work at a number of levels in order to meet the needs of students. In it we examine each aspect of the CLD bridge and explore the ways in which these need to be kept in balance in order for CLD to be effective. The different parts of the bridge are drawn from recent theory, policy and practice and point the way forward to the future of CLD. The chapter begins by introducing the concept of the CLD suspension bridge and how it operates, and then goes on to explore each aspect of the bridge and its relationship to CLD. This includes issues and trends that will shape people's understandings of career, including significant political questions about the future of work, and an examination of some recent theoretical approaches that describe the concept of career in a climate of perpetual change. The chapter concludes with a discussion of the challenges in balancing the tensions that enable the bridge to function.

The CLD bridge

The CLD bridge is a suspension bridge that functions because of tensions and stresses that are kept carefully in balance. Without these tensions, the bridge will simply collapse. We have chosen the metaphor of a suspension bridge because it depicts the tensions that CLD has experienced for many years – tensions which we believe will not disappear in the future. The metaphor is particularly useful as it harnesses these tensions. It interprets these tensions as challenging opportunities and possibilities rather than threats.

Figure 11.1 is a labelled diagram of a suspension bridge showing different aspects of the bridge's construction. The diagram shows the main forces at work in the suspension bridge, which keep it in place: tension in the cables, compression in the towers and the weight of the road. The cables pull in opposite directions in order to produce tension and the bridge is anchored into the ground by compression, which passes down through the towers. Weight is in turn transferred via the towers into the ground. The cables also hold up the road deck,

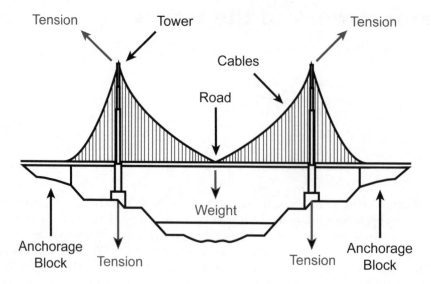

Figure 11.1 Suspension bridge

and the weight of the road deck is then transferred back from the cables to the towers and the anchorage blocks. This weight is in turn transferred via the towers into the ground.

The CLD bridge is built on principles of social constructivism and draws on recent theory, policy and practice in order to point the way forward for future practice. At this point, it is important to emphasise the metaphorical nature of the CLD bridge – it is accepted that it may not necessarily be wholly accurate from a technical perspective (Figure 11.2).

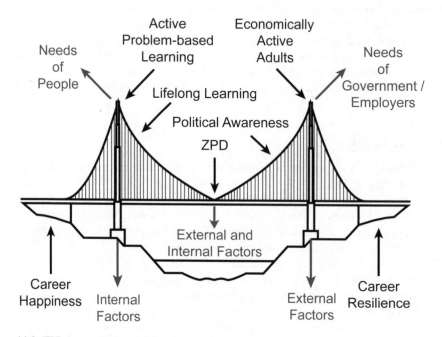

Figure 11.2 ZPD (zone of proximal development) bridge

Principles of social constructivism

In recent years, ideas about the term career have been changing in the following ways.

- In the past, career was seen as a job, or paid work, with some kind of progression. In other words, it was something concrete (an occupation, such as a carpenter or a hairdresser) that people could be matched to, or could match themselves to. This is often referred to as a positivist understanding of career and was suited to stable environments.
- In more recent years, as the idea of 'a job for life' has been questioned, people have begun to see career as a journey through life where they move from one area of work to the next, maybe with breaks in between. In addition, it is seen as their life as a whole, not just their paid work. This is often referred to as a constructivist understanding of career and is particularly relevant in times of change.

However, even though these terms are used in academic circles, whether or not young people see career like this is very doubtful. Many young people still think of career as 'what I am going to do when I leave school/in the future' and for most this will be linked firmly with their next step (a job, a course, etc.)

In one sense the CLD bridge spans the gap between education and work in it broadest definition. However, because of the constant and rapid changes in the world at large, the bridge operates with two-way traffic. This demonstrates the need for people to develop themselves continually, revisiting education (in the broad sense of learning) through continuing development, in order to meet their own needs and those of their employers, families and communities, thereby constructing career throughout their life course.

Constructivism is a term that is applied in many different academic and professional fields. In education, the type of constructivism that is most commonly referred to is social constructivism. Readers who are trained teachers will no doubt be familiar with some seminal work from this perspective by writers such as Vygotsky (1978), Bruner (1996) and Wood (1998).

First, it is important to consider what social constructivism means in relation to learning about career. Here are four key points:

- Knowledge about career is not something that people acquire. Students are not 'empty vessels' that you can 'fill up' with career information, assuming that they will then be able to make decisions.
- Knowledge about career is constructed through activity.
- Knowledge about career is constructed in interactions with others, including CLD professionals, other teachers, parents, peers and so on. Students need opportunities for discussion in order to construct new knowledge.
- People construct knowledge in their social and cultural context.

From the perspective of social constructivism, language performs a central role, as it is the means by which people interact and pass on culture and traditions through generations. Therefore, people develop *in* society and are immersed in and inseparable from their culture via processes of communication. However, society is not static, it changes as people question social practices (Bruner 1996).

We now explore each aspect of the CLD bridge.

Tensions and weight

On either side of the bridge there are two opposing tensions that, when kept in balance, keep the bridge in place and allow it to function well. On the left-hand side of the bridge are the needs of individual students; CLD is built on principles of student centredness and enabling people to lead satisfying lives by fulfilling their potential. However, on the opposite side are the needs of society more broadly, including the needs of government and employers. These also have to be met in order for society and the individuals within it to continue to prosper. At the centre of the bridge is the individual in their social context: self in society.

Anchorage blocks

On either side of the bridge there are anchorage blocks that prevent the bridge from collapsing due to the tensions pulling against one another in opposite directions.

Career happiness

On the left-hand side of the bridge, the anchorage block is represented by the concept of career happiness. Career happiness is focused on the individual and includes:

- Maintaining a healthy work/life balance. The phrase 'all work and no play' is well known and many young people are recognising the value of leading a balanced life, where work and leisure both have priority.
- Choosing a field of work that will be satisfying to the person concerned. This often involves making choices that are in tune with your values. These could be tangible extrinsic values (such as the importance of earning a high wage), more intangible intrinsic values (such as feeling respected for what I do) or lifestyle values (such as where I live and how far I travel to work).
- Working for an organisation that is in tune with your values. Many young people care about the environment and may want to work for companies who are careful about their carbon footprint. As part of this process, they may also be keen to support local businesses.

Career happiness can be seen as a composite of all of the five outcomes in *Every Child Matters* (see Chapter 3), with a particular focus on 'enjoy and achieve'.

The phrase 'the only constant is change', attributed to Heraclitus, is well known. We can only assume that the changes outlined in Chapter 1 will continue apace in the coming years as the impact of globalisation and information technology are fully realised. No doubt emerging economies, such as China, India and Brazil, will begin to play a more central role in world trade, which will affect job opportunities both here and abroad. The falling birth rate and rising life expectancy in the UK, alongside questions about the viability of pensions, will continue to demand that those capable of work are employed for longer, and so paid work that offers prospects of career happiness is likely to grow in importance.

Career resilience

The anchorage block on the right-hand side of the bridge is represented by career resilience. In a changing world, people will need to be resilient, having 'the capacity to deal with, or bounce back from, unexpected challenges or disappointments' (Canadian Career

Development Foundation 2007: 2). When seeking to define the term 'career resilience', Fourie and Van Vuuren (1998) found the following four factors to be particularly important:

• An underlying belief in oneself and one's abilities and skills.
• A disregard for traditional sources of career success, for example a high salary.
• A high level of self reliance.
• Being receptive to change, rather than fighting it or dismissing it.

A high level of career resilience will enable people to cope with turbulence in the labour market, as they experience such things as redundancy. More research is needed to find out how the term 'resilience' can be applied to CLD.

The cables

The cables on the CLD bridge take the weight of the bridge itself.

Lifelong learning

On the left-hand side of the bridge is the concept of lifelong learning, which enables individuals to keep pace with change and continue to develop. However, the question of how CLD can prepare young people for an uncertain future remains problematic. Is it enough to make sure that young people have a good range of transferable skills that they can take into any working situation? CLD has a role to play in embedding lifelong learning into the lives of young people, encouraging them to have a thirst for learning and achieving their potential. This needs to be modelled by CLD practitioners so that students understand the benefits of it.

Political awareness

On the right-hand side of the bridge are the needs of society as a whole, including the government and employers. It is important to understand that CLD operates in an overtly political arena as it is closely related to economic policy and pressures such as ensuring that we have a workforce that will enable us to remain competitive and maintain prosperity. As a result, it is linked closely to government agendas such as wealth creation during the Thatcher years or social inclusion under Blair. Since the 1980s, society has become increasingly individualised and now people are expected to take responsibility for their own lives rather than relying on others (e.g. the state) to do this for them. Education (including CLD) is no exception to this and in recent years we have witnessed a growth in personalised learning. Whether you are at school, college, university or out in the workplace, each individual is now expected to take charge of their own learning and development and to engage in a process of lifelong learning. Those who do not learn and develop, for whatever reason, risk being left behind in an ever-changing world.

Employers of the future will want to know that their employees will continue to learn and develop, in order to keep pace with change. They will also value staff who are adaptable and flexible, who have initiative and can look to the future. Gothard et al. (2001:89) recognise that career 'guidance will be required throughout life, rather than just at the entry to the labour market', but also point to the need for those involved in CLD to rethink the purpose of guidance in a world where the concept of career is unstable. It will also be important for those involved in CLD to be conversant with changes in the labour market, education policy and the curriculum.

The road

Spanning the bridge is the road, or the space between education and work. Professionals involved in CLD need to have a knowledge and understanding of theoretical approaches, such as those covered in Chapter 1. There is, of course, a very real need for theory to keep pace with change so that it remains useful. No one theory alone can offer everything we need to know and all theories develop over time as writers undertake more research and develop their ideas. As Law (1996: 50) rightly points out, 'theory reflects the field's conversation with itself, developing new questions which previous contributors have left unanswered'.

There is no doubt that traditional approaches (such as trait and factor matching) have aided those in CLD for many years and are valuable, but there is also a need for new approaches that fit twenty-first-century life. Otherwise, theory runs the risk of being seen as outdated at best and irrelevant at worst.

The road represents recent theoretical developments in careers work: 'my career narrative' from a constructivist perspective and the zone of proximal development from a social constructivist perspective.

My career narrative

Patton and McMahon (2006) make the following useful points about constructivism and career:

- people actively construct their understanding of career through their own thinking and action;
- while doing this, they interact with people around them;
- the process of learning about career is more important than the outcome;
- learning about career is a lifelong process and life is not lived in stages.

This lifelong process of constructing career is often done in story or narrative form and CLD professionals can offer support to students who are writing their career stories in a number of ways. For example:

- offering a safe and comfortable environment where students can express their hopes and desires freely and tell their story;
- listening carefully to the story being told;
- helping students to reflect on and process information in order to help them make meaning and 'script' possible futures;
- offering support in finding information.

Patton and McMahon (2006) have developed their Systems Theory Framework (STF) as a map to guide students who are constructing their own career development and the CLD professionals who are helping them. Other tools, such as Severy's (2008) online career narrative intervention, have been designed in order to help students to explore and reflect on such things as their skills, values and experiences. In the future it is likely that more such tools will be developed, and as yet, there is no teaching/learning programme of CLD for use in schools and colleges based on constructivist principles.

The zone of proximal development (ZPD)

When working with young people, there is a need for theory that is based on research and on what works in practice. The changes in the concept of career outlined above show that good careers work of the future will involve more than teaching job search skills such as writing a good CV and interview techniques. Approaches will be needed that help students and CLD professionals understand themselves and their futures in relation to their social context. In order for people to fulfil their potential, there will also be a need for a growing understanding of the ways in which people can develop as they construct their career in an ongoing way. In these respects, Vygotsky's (1978) ZPD is a very useful concept.

Wood (1998: 26) defines the ZPD as 'the gap that exists for an individual child (or adult) between what he is able to do alone, and what he (sic) can achieve with help from one more knowledgeable than himself'. Learning about career in the ZPD has the following characteristics:

- it is interactive and takes place by active participation in a social and cultural setting;
- the learner works in partnership with a more experienced person/people;
- learning focuses on active problem solving and participation (Lave and Wenger 1991);
- help and support are reduced as the learner constructs new knowledge and gains the required skills;
- the overall goal is independence.

Within the ZPD, the focus is on what the learner can do next (hence proximal) and the overall aim is that the learner becomes independent. Over time, help and support are reduced as the learner constructs new knowledge and gains the required skills. What the learner can do with help today, they will be able to do alone tomorrow.

A student in Bassot's (2006) research with sixth form students used a metaphor which usefully described the ZPD in the context of CLD. He used the term 'joining the dots' to describe how he envisaged his career. By this he meant the kinds of pictures children enjoy drawing by joining up sequentially numbered dots. He saw his career as an emerging picture that he was drawing (and no one else). The picture's title was 'me and my future', and was one that he would continue to draw throughout his life. His interview with the careers adviser helped him to find more dots in his picture (such as his options, his strengths and limitations) and to join them. The picture was complex and drawn in pencil, so that changes could easily be made with an eraser.

To summarise, learning about career in the ZPD needs to be active, and the student must be at the centre and involved at every stage of the process. The student will then construct new knowledge in relation to career *with* the CLD practitioner who withdraws their support over time as the student moves gradually towards independence. Young people need many opportunities to participate in career-related activities with discussion in order to construct knowledge about career.

All of the above assumes that access to the CLD bridge is open for all, which for some is not the case. Numbers of people on the margins of the labour market will need help in gaining access to the CLD bridge. For such individuals, the CLD bridge could be seen as a toll bridge, where CLD practitioners provide support for people to gain access onto the bridge via programmes of education and training.

The towers

The towers that support the bridge on either side ensure that the foundations of the bridge are firm and prevent the bridge from collapsing.

Active problem-based learning

On the left-hand side of the bridge are programmes of CLD that are designed on the social constructivist principles of active, problem-based experiential learning. These involve discussions and interactions with others which enable people to make progress within their ZPD. These are explored in more detail in the next chapter.

Independent economically active adults

On the right-hand side of the bridge are independent economically active adults who enable society to remain prosperous while continuing to develop themselves in a holistic sense.

Keeping the CLD bridge in balance – tensions and dilemmas

The CLD suspension bridge needs to be kept in balance in order to perform its function and also needs to be strong to resist stormy weather caused by turbulence in global economies. Being so closely linked with government agendas brings dilemmas for CLD professionals. CLD emphasises the rights of the individual to choose what they want to do; people are far more likely to achieve career happiness when they choose something that they enjoy and that is in tune with their values. But sometimes this will conflict with government policy that encourages everyone to stay in education and become economically active. This raises the question, 'Do people have a right not to participate?' What about those who do not wish to be economically active but who wish to pursue other life goals, such as volunteering or caring for a relative?

CLD practitioners often experience dilemmas when they are asked to promote government agendas that may not always be in the interests of their students. For example, as the curriculum in schools becomes more vocationalised, is it the job of CLD professionals to promote this? Many young people will not be ready at the age of 14 to make career decisions, but, depending on their academic achievement, they may be forced to do so. While it is not the role of CLD to promote government agendas, but to work in the interests of the people it serves, all CLD services need funding, much of which comes from government. CLD professionals need to become experts at gaining the trust of young people and keeping their wishes, hopes and desires at the centre despite pressure to fulfil government targets. By doing so, they will fulfil the requirements of the Education and Skills Act (OPSI 2008) for impartial career education.

There is no doubt that there is a clear statistical correlation between an individual gaining more qualifications and their earning power; those with qualifications have more choice and can progress further than those without (Roberts 2005). It is important that CLD challenges inequality in society rather than simply reinforcing it and it is clear that qualifications are not all that is required. Employers also need people who can be trained and develop the skills required to function well in the workplace such as communication skills, working in a team and self-management. Employability skills can be taught effectively in CLD, and by doing so CLD will form the vital bridge between education and work and ultimately a successful independent life. With well-developed CLD provision, a society with a qualified workforce is much more likely to be able to develop a highly skilled workforce. Whilst meeting the needs of employers is important, this is not the only consideration: it is important that the needs of young people are also kept in focus. This balance between fulfilling the needs of employers and young people keeps the CLD bridge in place and fulfilling its function.

Meeting the needs of individuals and social groups

Since its inception, career guidance has had an emphasis on working with those who are disadvantaged in some way. Similarly some of the best practice in careers education can be found in special schools, specifically designed for those who often struggle to gain entry to the labour market. The overall goal of CLD is to enable young people to lead 'successful' independent lives in the future. How one defines 'success' is ultimately up to the individual concerned, but we suggest that career happiness and career resilience are two key aspects of 'success'. Whilst we recognise that a small number of people in society may not be able to achieve independence, many will, and in order to bring this about, CLD has a strategic role to play in bringing social groups together in order to meet the needs of individuals.

For example, in any local area there will be schools, colleges, employers and training providers who can all help young people prepare for their future. Such organisations are described by Engeström (2001) as activity systems that can work together in order to meet the needs of the students. However, such organisations do not always have a local forum for meeting together and CLD professionals can play an active part in organising this. Such a forum will bring these organisations together in order to discuss how the needs of students can be met. This could include agreeing provision for work experience, finding out about job vacancies or new courses on offer locally. More importantly, such a forum will also keep those involved in CLD up to date with what is happening in their local labour market, and in particular what employers and training providers are looking for in their recruits.

Conclusion

The future is always difficult to predict, particularly when political agendas are involved. It is clear that holding the CLD bridge in place will be elusive and difficult. It will involve balancing the needs of students against those of employers and those who fund services such as the government. The IAG standards (DCSF 2007) are designed to fulfil this function, but it is questionable whether these will be enough. As local authorities come to the fore in managing services for young people again, career guidance services are increasingly being based in schools as well as being provided by outside organisations. Inevitably this will create challenges to the provision of impartial IAG.

Finally, after a period of time focused on supporting holistically those young people most at risk, the word 'career' seems to be coming back into fashion following the Leitch Review (2006) of skills which advocated a new universal careers service for adults. It is time for the professional identity of CLD professionals to be re-established and for all young people to be supported in reaching their career potential. How this can be done is the subject of the next chapter, where the practical aspects of the CLD bridge metaphor will be described and explained further.

Discussion points

1   How could your CLD programme help young people to achieve career happiness and career resilience?
2   What opportunities are there for students to develop their career narrative?
3   What activities could you provide to enable them to make progress within their ZPD?

References

Bassot, B. (2006) 'Constructing new understandings of career guidance: joining the dots', in H.L. Reid and J. Bimrose (eds.) *Constructing the Future: Transforming Career Guidance,* Stourbridge: Institute of Career Guidance.

Bruner, J.S. (1996) *The Culture of Education,* Cambridge, MA: Harvard University Press.

Canadian Career Development Foundation (2007) *Applying the Construct of Resilience to Career Development,* Montreal: Canadian Millennium Scholarship Foundation. Online: www.millennium-scholarships.ca/images/Publications/Resilience_2007-EN.pdf (accessed 12 February 2010).

DCSF (2007) *Quality Standards for Young People's Information Advice and Guidance (IAG),* Nottingham: DCSF Publications. Online: www.cegnet.co.uk/files/CEGNET0001/ManagingCEG/QualityStandardsforIAG/quality_standards_young_people.pdf (accessed 12 February 2010).

Engeström, Y. (2001) 'Expansive learning at work: toward an activity theoretical reconceptualization', *Journal of Education and Work,* 14(1): 133–156.

Fourie, C. and Van Vuuren, L.J. (1998) 'Defining and measuring career resilience', *Journal of Industrial Psychology,* 24(3): 52–59.

Gothard, B., Mignot, P., Offer, M. and Ruff, M. (2001) *Careers Guidance in Context,* London: Sage.

Lave, J. and Wenger, E. (1991) *Situated Learning: Legitimate Peripheral Participation,* Cambridge: Cambridge University Press.

Law, B. (1996) 'A career learning theory', in A.G. Watts, J. Killeen, J.M. Kidd and R. Hawthorn (eds.) *Re-thinking Careers Education and Guidance: Theory, Policy and Practice,* London: Routledge.

Leitch, S. (2006). *Prosperity for all in the Global Economy – World Class Skills,* Norwich: HMSO. Online: www.dfes.gov.uk/furthereducation/uploads/documents/2006-12%20LeitchReview1.pdf (accessed 13 February 2010).

OPSI (2008) Education and Skills Act 2008. Online: www.opsi.gov.uk/acts/acts2008/en/ukpgaen_20080025_en_1.htm (accessed 12 December 2010).

Patton, W. and McMahon, M. (2006) *Career Development and Systems Theory: Connecting Theory and Practice,* Rotterdam/Taipei: Sense Publishers.

Roberts, K. (2005) 'Social class, opportunity structures and career guidance', in B. Irving and B. Malik (eds.) *Critical Reflections on Career Education and Guidance: Promoting Social Justice within a Global Economy,* London: RoutledgeFalmer.

Severy, L. (2008) 'Analysis of an online career narrative intervention: "What's My Story?"', *Career Development Quarterly,* 56: 26–273.

Vygotsky, L.S. (1978) *Mind in Society,* Cambridge, MA: Harvard University Press.

Wood, D. (1998) *How Children Think and Learn,* 2nd edn, Oxford: Blackwell.

Chapter 12

Careers work of the future

The view from the bridge

In this final chapter we take a critical look at the future of careers work in schools and consider how innovation can improve it. In the previous chapter, we discussed the bridge as a new metaphor for CLD in schools. Here, we explore practical ways of using the ideas built into the bridge to transform CLD provision in schools.

Limited conceptions of CLD

Shortcomings in CLD provision in schools occur for a range of reasons and are a concern for key stakeholders as well as the profession and can include the following.

Over-reliance on information giving and insufficient emphasis on how to convert information into useful career knowledge

In terms of the *Looking Forward* (SCAA 1995) model of the aims of careers education (see Chapter 1), learning how, why and when to access careers information is a vital part of career exploration. The wider aspects of career exploration can be addressed through problem-based interactive learning as represented by the left-hand tower of the bridge.

Punctuated inputs linked to career matching at decision and transition points, at the expense of continuous and progressive CLD provision

The focus of this kind of careers work in schools is overwhelmingly on the next career goal or destination for the individual, and there is an over-dependence on computer-matching programs, the one-off guidance interview and making a decision. This kind of careers provision can look dynamic, busy and fun, but when scrutinised carefully is primarily about short-term procedural skills (e.g. CV writing, completion of UCAS forms and interview skills practice) rather than long-term essential skills for living, learning and earning. In relation to the CLD bridge, the traffic is one-way and the young person's development is missing the element of lifelong learning that involves two-way movement on the bridge.

A focus on a narrow view of economic well-being

This version of economic well-being is rooted in economic individualism and wealth creation. It reduces the meaning of career well-being to earning a living and contributing to national global competitiveness. Everett (2007) shows that the quest for personal autonomy and well-being can embrace a commitment to communitarian altruism and environmental responsibility. Balancing and reconciling the needs of the individual with the needs of society is reflected in the tensions in the cables of the bridge.

A naïve optimism about the power of individual agency to enable young people to transform their circumstances

Some enterprising young people will succeed in overcoming the barriers they face, but many individuals and groups need strong networks of support to help them improve their situation. The bridge has a focus on personal agency and the development of the skills needed for lifelong learning and career resilience – a career is after all a self-managed concept – but it balances this with a concern for career as a social interaction and a socially enabled condition. The argument is that schools can and should do more to get young people onto the bridge. This does not negate the part played by 'happenstance' (chance and serendipity) in career development. Even though it is largely outside anyone's control, it is important that young people learn how to recognise unexpected opportunities and how to take advantage of them. The structure of the bridge is built to cope with the unpredictable weather around it. The application of chaos theory to career development is also starting to attract attention (Pryor 2005).

A one-dimensional view of CLD

The dominant career development paradigm in schools is concerned with unlocking potential – helping the individual to become everything that they can become. School CLD programmes do not often explore the discourse of career as it is understood in employment settings. This discourse is about the career development of individuals in the organisation and how to improve their work performance and job satisfaction through career discussions, appraisal, acceleration programmes and succession planning. Starting points for interested readers include Arnold (1997), Arthur *et al.* (1999), Baruch (2004), Hirsh *et al.* (2001), Peiperl *et al.* (2000) and Peiperl *et al.* (2002). Rather than polarise these two positions, the twin towers of the bridge recognise that individuals have multiple identities, roles and understandings. They can and do hold different meanings of 'career' and 'work' in their minds.

A narrow skills-based view of CLD

The focus on equipping young people with the skills that employers are looking for fails to do justice to the wider view of CLD – that it is about enabling young people to find meaningful work where they can deploy their work-related skills in a way which is consistent with their interests and values. CLD professionals are reluctant to breach their code of impartiality by promoting one set of values over another, but this dilemma can be avoided by providing opportunities for learners to clarify and take ownership of their own values.

Elements of the bridge in practice

With reference to the description of the bridge in Chapter 11, we now explore practical learning opportunities which relate to specific elements of the structure.

Tensions and weight: the needs of the individual and the needs of society

In the model described in Chapter 11, the tension of the cables and the weight of the bridge are in dynamic equilibrium. They represent the tension between the needs of individuals and the needs of society. How can we help young people to explore this tension and how their choices relate to it? The following topics suggest ways of meeting the needs of individuals while recognising that ultimately careers are socially sanctioned.

Why do we work?

Hold a group session that looks at the benefits and drawbacks of employment. Concepts such as identity, status, fame and worth can be explored by posing questions such as:

- Why do people give up financially rewarding careers for less well-paid jobs?
- Why do people volunteer their time and skills in communities?
- Why do lottery winners continue to work in some way?
- What are the advantages and disadvantages of running your own business rather than working for someone else?

Who am I to you?

Discuss in small groups the different roles individuals might have in their lifetimes and relate the different roles to different life stages. In collaboration with citizenship staff, discuss the different relationships we have with other people and the different skills we use in the various roles we play. Introduce the concept of 'interdependence' and discuss how everyone is dependent on everyone else for the sustainability of their jobs and communities.

The changing nature and future of work

In collaboration with staff in the history department and perhaps the local library, museum or newspaper, organise a project on the changing labour market in your area over the past 200 years. Consider work socialisation, the opportunity structure, the decline and rise of different occupations, the experiences of different groups (e.g. women) and family work histories.

Selling myself

This is an opportunity to consider the notion of the labour market as a market place where what is on offer is subject to changes in supply and demand. Students consider how they might attract a 'buyer' for their skills and qualities. They think about how they can keep up to date with what the 'market' needs by investing in training, education and experience. They learn the importance of managing their online identities (e.g. on social networking sites) as an extension of the self-presentation skills they use when applying for jobs.

Think globally

Collaboration with economics and business studies staff could be useful in helping young people understand the impact of globalisation on their labour market opportunities. Globalisation has impacted on the movement of money, people, goods and services around the world, so that even local labour markets are affected by changes on the other side of the globe. Depending on the age, ability and interests of the group, the impact of globalisation can be investigated through case studies of small and medium-sized enterprises (SMEs) and large multinational corporations. Learners can devise their own questions and do their research using the internet, telephone, company brochures or even visits. They can follow this up by considering the skills and qualities that employers require and how they can acquire them.

Green and sustainable careers

Individuals may express concern for the environment but do not necessarily think through the implications for their own careers. Green jobs are those that make an appreciable contribution to maintaining or restoring environmental quality and avoid future damage to the Earth's ecosystems. However, sustainable living will require the greening of all jobs in the future. Possible investigations include:

- How will I be affected by green and sustainable careers?
- What kinds of jobs will decline and what kinds of jobs will be boosted by climate change over the next 5–10 years?
- What will sustainable development mean for jobs in the public and private sectors ten years from now?
- Choose a job and suggest how you could transform it to leave a smaller carbon footprint.
- How can we achieve 'sustainable well-being for all' and how will it change people's working lives?

Career entrepreneurs

Enterprising skills and attitudes are a pre-requisite for self-managed careers. Business games and simulations can help young people to appreciate the part that risk-taking, creativity, problem-solving, a can-do attitude, energy and determination play in managing their own careers. Enterprise activities also help young people to appreciate the part that initiative and enterprise play in economic life, and that self-employment is an option for them. It is important to give young people experience of different kinds of mini-enterprise; for example, share-holder companies, cooperatives and social enterprises. Entrepreneurs can be a source of inspiration to young people. Organisations that run start-up schemes for small businesses will help you find new entrepreneurs for your students to interview.

Criminal investigations

Work is one of the principal ways that individuals interact with society. The opportunities, requirements and expectations of government, society, employers, communities and families impinge greatly on the careers that individuals can have. Investigating criminal careers opens up a rich seam of possibilities. Do criminal careers (e.g. pirate, gang leader) confer the same benefits on individuals as legitimate careers? Why does society try to prevent individuals from having criminal careers? How do some work cultures become corrupt and what can be done about it?

STEMming the flow

The government, universities and employers in the science, technology, engineering and maths (STEM) sectors have become concerned about the decline in young people choosing STEM subjects, courses and careers. Young people could take part in the range of activities developed by STEM agencies for the national STEM programme (www.dcsf.gov.uk/stem/). Learners' acquisition of STEM-related knowledge, skills and attitudes benefits individuals, society and the economy.

Anchorage blocks: career happiness and resilience

Career happiness, as we discussed in Chapter 11, is rooted in the concept of meaningful work. According to Henderson (1999–2000), career happiness results when individuals find or develop careers that allow them to express their core identities and values. Career resilience and adaptability are vital too for career well-being (Canadian Careers Development Foundation 2007). Preparing young people for growth and change is more important than teaching them how to make a decision (van Vianen et al. 2009). In fact, we need to use better models of decision-making (see Hodkinson 2009; Hemsley-Brown and Foskett 2002; and Foskett 2004 for a discussion of career decision-making by young people). The following topics suggest ways of strengthening young people's career resilience and promoting their career happiness.

Career values

Values clarification exercises are an important way of taking career learning to a deeper level (Barnes 2008). Card-sort activities using cards with different values written on them will help individuals to:

- list the values that are most important to them;
- identify contradictory values;
- identify the values that it would be most useful to have for doing a particular job;
- recognise that people have different value systems;
- reflect on the values that underpinned a previous career decision that they made.

Career needs

Maslow's (1943) hierarchy of five levels of need also sheds light on how individuals may define career happiness in different ways. At the highest level in the hierarchy, career happiness is linked to self-actualisation. Individuals discuss the needs that can be met by the careers they have chosen.

Happenstance

Discuss the part that 'happenstance' (taking advantage of unexpected or chance events) plays in career happiness. Students research happenstance in people's lives through biography and fiction. They imagine a future episode in their own lives.

Finding the hole in the heart

Discussion of the part played by emotional intelligence (Goleman 1997) in career success opens up a wide range of issues such as feminisation of the workplace, leadership and effective participation. Savickas refers to career choices as being a process of 'finding the hole in the heart' and then the various options for filling it. His proposed questioning techniques for guidance interviews (Savickas 2006) ask the client about early childhood memories, role models and favourite books and films. The purpose is to establish, not so much the best fit for the skills and qualities of the individual, but the best fit for the emotional fulfilment offered by different career opportunities.

Am I really living the way I want to live?

In collaboration with RE staff, discuss with learners the relationships between spirituality, religion and career development.

- How does faith impact on career decision self-efficacy, career values and job satisfaction?
- What is the meaning of work in people's lives?
- What do the major religions say about 'suitable' or 'right' work?
- How do the major religions view money, materialism and happiness?

Faith issues in career development are explored by Fox (2003), Duffy (2006) and Hambly (2009).

The future of careers

How predictable and random are careers? Forecasts that, on average, young people will have between six and ten changes of job in their lifetimes suggest that we should prepare them for a volatile and uncertain future. Investigations based on issues such as this can lead to very interesting and rewarding career learning:

- Investigate future of work and career scenarios; for example, Watts (1996), Offer (2005).
- Investigate how Pryor (2005) has tried to apply chaos theory to career development, using terms such as 'strange attractors', 'turbulence', 'sensitivity to initial conditions' and 'information load'.
- Identify typical career patterns for groups such as young offenders, footballers and civil servants; and use case studies of individual career trajectories to show how seemingly random events can disrupt otherwise inevitable career patterns.

Cables: lifelong learning and political awareness

The cables of the CLD bridge represent two critical concepts: lifelong learning and political awareness. These elements are essential in order to hold up the weight of the bridge and allow traffic to pass over it. In order for young people to travel across the bridge between learning and work, and return as many times as they need to, lifelong learning and an awareness of the politics of lifelong learning and work are essential. Lifelong learning is a contested concept (Mojab 2009) and individuals need to be aware of the difficulties they may have to overcome in order to secure the benefits of lifelong learning for themselves and, perhaps, for others. The following topics will help learners understand why lifelong learning is important and relevant to them, what skills they need to gain access to opportunities, what the benefits may be and what support CLD professionals can give them:

A learning plan

Introduce your students to the idea of maintaining an individual learning plan (ILP). Start by critiquing the idea that it is important to engage in lifelong learning. It may be obvious to individuals who expect to work in the high-skill sectors of the economy, but what about those who expect to be working in the often invisible, low-skill, informal and survival sectors of the local labour market? Brainstorm practical (and magical) examples of lifelong learning so that the term does not become a meaningless mantra. Show students a template for an ILP. Be prepared to discuss in whose best interest the ILP has been designed for – Does it meet the needs of the school, the individual or both? Include a section in the ILP for learners to analyse the risks associated with their plan. Risk analysis is a skill learners will need throughout life. Explain that investing in your own learning can incur financial costs (e.g. fees, materials, transport, loss of income), time costs (e.g. loss of leisure) and emotional costs (e.g. less time with family and friends). What is the likely 'return on investment' from their plan? Also include sections for learners to record sources of support for carrying out their plan, what their goals are and the steps they need to take to achieve them.

Lifelong learning investigations

Use a case study approach to enable learners to gain insights into the meaning and relevance of lifelong learning and the political agendas shaping current provision. Possible topics for case studies could include:

- Critically review an organisation's policy on lifelong learning – for example, induction, mentoring, employee development programmes (for some or for all?). (This could be completed as a work experience assignment.)
- Investigate the impact of lifelong learning policies on the position of women in sectors such as construction and the built environment.
- Evaluate the impact of the Ford EDAP (Employee Development and Assistance Programme) and other lifelong learning initiatives run by Ford at Dagenham.
- Find out how the 'unionlearn programme' (www.unionlearn.org.uk/) aims to help unions to become lifelong learning organisations and to spread the lifelong learning message to all union members.
- Examine the contribution of Foundation Degrees which combine academic study with workplace learning to improve career development opportunities for people already in work.
- Investigate what adult and community learning is for and how it is changing.
- Find out about and assess the impact of family learning projects in your area where children and parents learn together.
- Write a case study report of the workings and achievements of an informal learning/self-help group known to you – for example, women's or ethnic minority groups.

Lifelong learning

Chapman and Aspin (1997) describe the 'triadic' nature of lifelong learning. They propose that such learning benefits the individual in their personal self-realisation, the economy in its ability to respond to a rapidly changing labour market, and society in the maintenance of the cultural 'glue' with which traditions and creative arts maintain communities of all ethnic origins.

In small groups, learners could be asked to think of examples in each of the three aspects of lifelong learning. For example:

- learning a foreign language or a musical instrument (personal self-realisation);
- IT, customer service or management training in the work place (the economy);
- training to be a school governor or singing in a choir (society).

It might be that there are many overlaps, which illustrates the possibility that learning in one context can be beneficial in many others.

Extended services

Are our schools, colleges and workplaces equipped or prepared for the 'returning traffic' on the bridge? Extended services, which were formerly 'extended schools' (Barnes and Chant 2008), offer a structure for providing such opportunities, but involvement in extended services activities for this purpose may be beyond the capacity of some schools. However, we can help to engage young people in wider learning so that they fully expect their journey across their bridge to be a round trip or even a series of round trips. Moreover, we can engage with the parents and carers of those young people to ensure that they also understand the long-term process of lifelong learning for lifelong career development. Possibilities include:

- after-school careers clubs designed to raise aspirations and challenge stereotyping;
- family learning;
- information sessions for parents/carers on their children's learning and career choices.

UK Youth Parliament

Young people themselves can be change-agents for CLD and lifelong learning through forums such as the student council in your school, local youth council or the UK Youth Parliament (www.ukyouthparliament.org.uk/). Areas of concern debated by the UK Youth Parliament have included the cost of bus travel and university tuition fees. Student forums can be used to give young people a voice on matters that affect them deeply including CLD provision and the curriculum offer.

Volunteering

The *Youth Matters* Green Paper (DfES 2005) encouraged young people to engage in volunteering as a way of improving their participation in the community and society in general, but also as a way of broadening their horizons and developing their skills and confidence. But what do we mean by volunteering? Putting this question to a group of students can encourage them to re-visit ideas about 'What is work?', 'Why work?' and 'Why volunteer?' The group could be asked to list voluntary 'jobs' that they know about, such as parents who help in the school or who coach sports in their spare time. Do they know about voluntary jobs such as being a magistrate or member of the House of Lords? Why might these jobs be better done by volunteers than by paid professionals? They could be asked to list the benefits for the volunteer such as getting work experience, meeting different people and 'giving something back to the community'. Ask students to find out about volunteering opportunities in the school, college or local community. These might be linked to schemes such as the Duke of Edinburgh's Award or the web-based 'Do-it' organisation that lists opportunities by postcode. Vinspired connects 16 to 25 year olds with volunteering opportunities in England (http://vinspired.com/about-us).

The road: career narrative

In Chapter 11, the road between the two sides of the bridge is described as representing the career narrative of an individual supported by lifelong learning. The use of narrative in CLD and guidance provision is an emerging option for practitioners. Internationally, it is strongly associated with the 'life-designing' model for career interventions (Savickas *et al.* 2009) and in England with staff associated with the Centre for Career and Personal Development (Edwards 2003; Reid 2009). The following topics tap into the rich seam of career narrative:

Famous biographies

One of the questions that Savickas asks in Life-Design Counselling is about the client's hero or role model. This might be a fictitious character such as Robin Hood or a real-life legend such as Nelson Mandela. Comparing ourselves with others need not be judgemental but can elicit questions such as 'What would I have done if I had been in that situation?' By taking a look at the stories behind well-known characters, young people have the opportunity to think about the choices that were made and what the consequences were. Choose a variety of characters from history, fiction and those currently in the news. Who do the students admire and why? What are the qualities of these people that are worth emulating? You might include individuals who have become well known for less than admirable reasons, or perhaps through 'happenstance' or serendipity.

My Story

After your learners have taken part in the previous exercise, invite them to tell their own story so far. Clearly this should be done with sensitivity, and if necessary only shared with a partner or friend rather than the rest of the group. Activities include:

- What are their earliest memories? Can they identify any themes or patterns in these early memories that help them to understand who and where they are today?
- What have been the challenges that have been overcome (such as settling into a new school) and what skills and qualities have been developed through those experiences? What have they found out about themselves in terms of their strengths and the things that they find difficult?
- What different versions of our own story do we tell and why do we do this?
- What other 'voices' are present in their stories? Why are they there?

If, for a range of reasons this exercise is likely to be challenging or raise sensitive issues, an alternative would be to tell their story from now to 35 years old. What are the decisions to be made and the consequences? What are the challenges and difficulties? How do we get from one chapter of our lives to another? These stories can be told, written or acted out. In collaboration with staff in the English and Drama departments, small groups might be tasked with writing a short story that incorporates all their stories, which is then acted out to the rest of the group.

Writer's block

Savickas (2006) uses the metaphor of storytelling to enable individuals to understand their career path to date (i.e. to make meaning and construct a view of themselves) and to help them 'write the next chapter' (i.e. make a decision about a direction or opportunity). Savickas describes how an individual who is not clear about their choice has, in effect, 'writer's block'. The practitioner's role here is as a writing coach, helping to look back at the story so far and to work out what that tells the individual about their next best step or choice. Case studies of other people's stories enable the learner to consider whether the case study is 'someone like me', thereby enabling them to learn from the safety of a third person.

Mentoring

The strategy for young people's IAG from the DCSF (2009) envisaged an expansion of mentoring schemes for young people, additional resources and research to identify good practice. Mentoring schemes vary widely: from individual to group mentoring, from peer mentors to business mentors and from mentoring for some (e.g. for under-attaining and/or disadvantaged students) to mentoring for all. Mentors can help young people to tell more positive versions of their own stories, but schools need to be aware of the difficulties and issues that their mentoring schemes can present (see Miller 2002; Colley 2006).

The road: ZPD

The ZPD provides a helpful overarching construct in relation to CLD and usefully describes some of the ways in which young people can make progress in their thinking about the complex and abstract issues related to career. The focus of learning in the ZPD is on the next steps: what learners can do with help today, they will be able to do alone tomorrow. Learning must be active, with a high level of student involvement, and interactive with lots of opportunities for discussion and reflection. Learners need support, but support that is withdrawn in a timely manner to help them move at their own speed towards independence. Possible approaches include the following:

Enabling parents

Without being consciously aware of it sometimes, parents listen to their child thinking out loud and gauge what the child understands, so that they can guide their child's thinking to a more advanced level of knowledge and understanding. This is most effective if the child learns more than they would be able to on their own. In the same way, young people can develop their career thinking with the help of their parents, if their parents have sufficient knowledge and skills to guide their child's learning. Schools can stimulate this process by:

- e-mailing parents to let them know about careers activities and events for their children;
- providing tips for parents on how to help their child choose what to study at options time and how to get the most out of events such as careers conventions and work experience;
- informing parents of changes to the education system and labour market so that what they talk to their children about is accurate and up to date.

Structured dialogic teaching

Students have limited access to one-to-one careers teaching and one-to-one guidance, and whole-class teaching does not lend itself easily to 'scaffolding' learning for individual learners (Wood 1998). However, these are not the only ways of organising learning in the classroom. Focus group teaching enables the careers teacher or careers adviser to concentrate on one group while other groups in the class are working independently on tasks that they have been given to do. The focus group benefits from the opportunity to extend their talk and their thinking, especially if the teacher or adviser is using the technique of 'dialogic teaching'. Alexander's (2006) principles of dialogic teaching are:

- teachers and learners address learning tasks together as a group rather than in isolation;
- teachers and learners listen to each other, share ideas and consider alternative viewpoints;
- learners articulate their ideas freely, without fear of embarrassment over 'wrong' answers, and they help each other to reach common understandings;
- teachers and learners build on their own and each other's ideas and chain them into coherent lines of thinking and enquiry;
- teachers plan and facilitate dialogic teaching with particular educational goals in view.

Another way of organising learning in the classroom is for the teacher to mediate the learning task for one group who then mediate the learning for their peers in group-work – that is, learner-to-learner mediation.

Interactive spaces

Social network learning presents new possibilities for structuring learning on the principles of the ZPD. Students' unmediated use of online careers software and resources can yield disappointing results. Career learning can be improved when students are supported by a more experienced adult or by their peers. Examples include:

- preparing learners to use a program or website, structuring their learning tasks and debriefing them afterwards;
- designing WebQuests (online enquiry-based projects);
- facilitating the writing of a careers wiki by the class;
- organising students' reflections on their career learning in the form of individual blogs;
- creating an online careers forum for students to collectively review what they have learnt from doing a careers project;
- making careers podcasts;
- placing e-learning careers modules in the careers room of the school's virtual learning environment (VLE) or learning platform.

The towers: active problem-based learning

In Chapter 11, we discussed the part that CLD programmes, designed on the social constructivist principles of active, problem-based, experiential learning, play in preparing young people for lifelong career well-being and happiness, and we have already articulated in Chapter 6 the teaching and learning methods that support this approach. Here are some further ideas.

Experiential learning

Experiential learning such as work experience learning is at its best transformative. The learning is intense, rich in interpretation and life changing. Although the learning is open-ended, it is set up in a controlled way to allow young people to learn by trial and error in a relatively risk-free way. Developments in ICT enable us to design virtual learning experiences for students that take these ideas a step further. Students can set up their own businesses on Second Life (http://secondlife.com/) and become an entrepreneur. Virtual careers fairs have been held on Second Life too. Career games and simulations are in their infancy but they will extend the possibilities of virtual experiential career learning.

Career trails

Year 9 pupils at a north London school experienced mobile or hand-held learning using PDA/smartphones to guide them on a careers and industry trail in their local area. They used the phones camera and audio recorder to interview commuters at King's Cross and staff at a nearby IT company. They recorded tasks using the touch screens on their phones. When they returned to school, they were able to use the data to make PowerPoint presentations about what they had learned. This activity has been filmed for TeachersTV (www.teachers.tv/video/24422).

Inquiry and problem-based learning

Presenting learners with a problem that needs to be solved develops creative and transferable learning skills. This works best when learners are able to draw on their previous experience, engage in interesting research and use the solution to help them in their own lives. Projects focusing on improving career transitions form a key area in CLD:

- Year 7 pupils could make recommendations to the school on how to improve the primary–secondary transition arrangements for Year 6 pupils.
- 14 to 19 year olds could investigate young people's experiences of their first few days in a new job and create a pack with advice for school leavers.

The towers: independent economically active adults

Helping young people to become independent economically active adults who continue to grow and develop through life is a key part of the CLD bridge. (Readers interested in accessing the literature on the career learning and development of adults could begin by visiting the websites of organisations such as NICEC, NIACE, IES and TAEN.) Helping young people to develop a perspective on adult careers and working life is important. Possible approaches include the following.

Issues-based career learning

Contemporary issues related to adult careers and working life are reported in the media daily. Features about issues such as the long hours culture, ageism and flexible working can trigger interesting discussions in tutor group meetings, and at the start of lessons about the needs of individuals and the needs of society, and what can and should be done to improve people's career resilience and well-being. Some students will have first-hand experience of difficult issues such as the effects of unemployment, workplace accidents or excessive work stress on a parent, so this kind of careers work needs to be handled sensitively.

Career stages

Ideas about stages of career development can stimulate young people's thinking about their goals and ambitions in life. Students could complete an activity based on Super's (1980) life-roles rainbow to better understand the concept of life-work balance; for example, http://oregoncis.uoregon.edu/pdf/curriculum/Life_Roles_Rainbow_MS. pdf. They could follow this up by critiquing the idea of career stages; for example, 'How well do Super's stages describe the experience of career development for women who do not pursue careers in large organisations?'

Final thoughts

In the first part of this book, we examined the theoretical, research and policy perspectives that underpin current CLD practice. The purpose of these chapters was to provide revelatory insights into the ways things are done. The middle part of the book focused on the ideas and explanations that would help careers professionals to lead, manage and provide CLD activities more effectively. 'Possibilities', the theme of the final part of the book, used the metaphor of the CLD bridge to explain our ideas for emerging or next practice, but we were under no illusions that for some readers this could be a bridge too far and the scope for transforming their CLD provision might be limited, at least for now. However, we also felt that even if schools could only embark on small changes to their CLD provision now, this could have considerable long-term effects. We hope that some of the ideas in this book, like the ripple effect of the flapping wings of a small butterfly, will help you make a big difference to the future lives of young people.

Discussion points

1   'Careers work in the future needs to be more sophisticated than it has been up to now.' What does this mean for CLD programmes in the future?
2   What teaching and learning activities based on the principles of the CLD bridge have you found to be most effective in enhancing the CLD of the young people you work with?

References

Alexander, R.J. (2006) *Towards Dialogic Teaching*, 3rd edn, York: Diaglos.

Arnold, J. (1997) *Managing Careers into the 21st Century*, London: Paul Chapman Publishing.

Arthur, M.B., Inkson, K. and Pringle, J.K. (1999) *The New Careers: Individual Action and Economic Change*, London: Sage.

Barnes, A. (2008) 'The role of values', *CEIAG Support Programme*. Online: www.cegnet.co.uk/files/CEGNET0001/briefings/Teaching%20about%20career%20values.pdf (accessed 13 February 2010).

Barnes, A and Chant, A. (2008) 'The place of guidance within the extended schools agenda – is spontaneity sufficient?', in H. Reid (ed.) *Constructing a Way Forward: Innovation in Theory and Practice for Career Guidance*. Canterbury: Canterbury Christ Church University, Centre for Career and Personal Development.

Baruch, Y. (2004) *Managing Careers: Theory and Practice*, Harlow: Pearson Education.

Canadian Career Development Foundation (2007) *Applying the Construct of Resilience to Career Development: Lessons in Curriculum Development*, Montreal: Canada Millennium Scholarship Foundation. Online: www.millenniumscholarships.ca/images/Publications/Resilience_2007-EN.pdf (accessed 13 February 2010).

Chapman, J.D. and Aspin, D.N. (1997) *The School, the Community and Lifelong Learning*, London: Cassell.

Colley, H. (2006) 'Mentoring in career guidance and career development: problems in formalising an informal practice?', *Career Research & Development* 14: 16–18.

DCSF (2009) *Quality, Choice and Aspiration. A Strategy for Young People's Information, Advice and Guidance*. Online: www.publications.dcsf.gov.uk/eOrderingDownload/IAG-Report-V2.pdf (accessed 12 February 2010).

DfES (2005a) *Youth Matters*, Nottingham: DfES Publications. Online: http://publications.dcsf.gov.uk/eOrderingDownload/Cm6629.pdf (accessed 18 February 2010).

Duffy, R.D. (2006) 'Spirituality, religion and career development: current status and future directions', *Career Development Quarterly*, 55(1): 52–63.

Edwards, A. (ed.) (2003) *Challenging Biographies: Re-locating the Theory and Practice of Careers Work*, Canterbury: Canterbury Christ Church University, Centre for Career and Personal Development.

Everett, M. (2007) *Making a Living While Making a Difference: Conscious Careers in an Era of Interdependence*, Gabriola Island, BC: New Society Publishers.

Foskett, N. (2004) *The Influence of the School on Young People's Decisions to Participate in Learning Post 16* RR538, London: DCSF.

Fox, L.A. (2003) 'The role of the church in career guidance and development: a review of the literature 1960–early 2000s', *Journal of Career Development*, 24(3): 167–182.

Goleman, D. (1997) *Emotional Intelligence: Why it an Matter More than IQ*, London: Bloomsbury.

Hambly, L. (2009) 'The courage of confidence: the role of faith in career choice', in H. Reid (ed.) *Constructing the Future: Career Guidance for Changing Contexts*, Stourbridge: Institute of Career Guidance. Online: www.icg-uk.org/c2/uploads/4%20liane%20hambly.pdf (accessed 13 February 2010).

Hemsley-Brown, J. and Foskett, N. (2002) 'Patterns of choice: a model of choice and decision-making', *Career Research & Development*, 6: 24–29.

Henderson, S.J. (1999–2000) 'Career happiness: More fundamental than job satisfaction', *Career Planning and Adult Development Journal*, 15(4): 5–10.

Hirsh, W., Jackson, C. and Kidd, J.M. (2001) *Straight Talking: Effective Career Discussions at Work*, NICEC Project Report, Cambridge: CRAC.

Hodkinson, P. (2009) 'Understanding career decision-making and progression: careership revisited', *Career Research & Development*, 21: 4–17.

Maslow, A. (1943) 'A theory of human motivation', *Psychological Review*, 50(4): 370–396.

Miller, A. (2002) *Mentoring Students and Young People: A Handbook of Effective Practice*, London: Kogan Page.

Mojab, S. (2009) 'Turning work and lifelong learning inside out: A Marxist-feminist attempt', in L. Cooper and S. Walters (eds.) *Learning/Work: Turning Work and Lifelong Learning Inside Out*, Cape Town: HSRC Press.

Offer, M. (ed) (2005) 'The future of work and career: an overview of the debate', *Career Research & Development*, 13: 2–6.

Peiperl, M., Arthur, M. and Anand, N. (eds.) (2002) *Career Creativity: Explorations in the Remaking of Work*, Oxford: Oxford University Press.

Peiperl, M., Arthur, M., Goffee, R. & Morris, T. (eds.) (2000) *Career Frontiers: New Conceptions of Working Lives*, Oxford: Oxford University Press.

Pryor, R.G. (2005) 'The Chaos Theory of Careers: a user's guide', *Career Development Quarterly*. Online: www.allbusiness.com/human-resources/careers-career-development/463087-1.html (accessed 13 February 2010).

Reid, H.L. (2009) 'Try something new – A narrative approach for career guidance: moving from theory into practice', *Career Guidance Today*, 17(1): 24–27.

Savickas, M. (2006) *Career Counseling (DVD)*, Washington, DC: American Psychological Association.

Savickas, M.L., Nota, L., Rossier, J., Dauwalder, J-P., Duarte, M.E., Guichard, J., Soresi, S., Van Esbroeck, R. and Van Vianen, A.E.M. (2009) 'Life designing: A paradigm for career construction in the 21st century', *Journal of Vocational Behaviour*, 75(3): 239–250.

SCAA (1995) *Looking Forward: Careers Education and Guidance in the Curriculum*, London: SCAA.

Super, D.E. (1980) 'Vocational adjustment: implementing a self-concept', *Career Development Quarterly*, 36: 188–194.

Van Vianen, A., De Pater, I. and Preenen, P. (2009) 'Adaptable careers: maximizing less and exploring more', *Career Development Quarterly*. Online: www.entrepreneur.com/tradejournals/article/201946687.html (accessed 13 February 2010).

Watts, A.G. (1996) *Careerquake*, DEMOS. Online: www.demos.co.uk/files/careerquake.pdf?1240939425 (accessed 13 February 2010).

Wood, D. (1998) *How Children Think and Learn*, 2nd edn, Oxford: Blackwell.

Index